Nonprofit Financial Oversight

The Concise and Complete Guide
for Boards and Finance Committees

Michael E. Batts, CPA

Accountability *Press*

in cooperation with

www.nonprofitcpa.com

Copyright © 2017 Michael E. Batts
All rights reserved

ISBN-13: 978-1974634200
ISBN-10: 1974634205

DEDICATION

This book is dedicated to Dan Busby. Dan Busby is a man of deep faith whose tireless efforts have made the world of financial accountability for nonprofit organizations much, much better – particularly in the area of Christian nonprofit organizations. A gifted CPA, Dan brings not only financial expertise to his work, but deep wisdom and passion to his calling. He is also one of the most genuinely positive people you could ever know – and he remains so, no matter what challenge comes his way. Dan Busby is one of those people we all want (or should want) to be more like. I have worked together with Dan for a number of years to advance the cause of financial accountability. That is truly a high honor and privilege.

Mike Batts

Acknowledgments

_____ - - _____

I would like to thank my CPA firm partners for their invaluable contributions, suggestions, and edits in connection with this book. Kim Morrison, Michele Wales, Mike Lee, and Julie James – thank you! It is a privilege to work alongside you as we strive to serve nonprofit organizations with excellence. I would also like to thank the members of my Communications Team who provided the critical logistical assistance in bringing this book to production. I would like to especially thank my son, Christopher Batts, for his excellent work in formatting, editing, and otherwise creating the finished product from the raw manuscript.

_____ - - _____

I also want to especially thank my wonderful and most lovely wife, Karen, for her continuous support and patience throughout the process of my writing this and other works. Her support has helped and inspired me every step of the way. Karen shares my hope that the sacrifice and work that has gone into writing this book will help nonprofit organizations be better and stronger...and more effective in making a lasting difference in the lives of people.

CONTENTS

INTRODUCTION

— - - —

You're Too Busy for Filler, Fluff, and Hooey.

Board and finance committee members are too busy for filler, fluff, and hooey... so this book doesn't contain any of that, with the possible exception of this paragraph. We'll get right to the point and we'll stay on point.

What This Book Is and Is Not

This book is a very concise guide for nonprofit board and finance committee members to aid them in carrying out their legal and fiduciary duty of financial oversight for their nonprofit organization. This book is not a financial operations guide for management. For leaders who are looking for a guide to financial operations for nonprofit organizations, I suggest that you consider my book *Church Finance – The Complete Guide to Managing Ministry Resources*, which I co-authored with attorney Richard Hammar. Notwithstanding its title, the vast majority of the content of that book is also applicable to non-church and non-religious nonprofit organizations.

Who Can Use This Book as a Guide?

This book is designed to help boards, finance committees, and anyone else charged with financial oversight of a nonprofit organization. It is my hope that officers, audit committees, investment committees, and others in a financial oversight role will find it helpful.

What Is Financial Oversight?

The term "financial oversight" is intended to mean just that...oversight, not management. As I described in my book, *Board Member Orientation – The Concise and Complete Guide to Nonprofit Board Service*, a nonprofit

1

organization's board has full authority over and responsibility for overseeing the affairs of the nonprofit organization. That does not mean, of course, that the board must carry out all the work of the organization. In fact, the board should not normally be involved at all in the operational activities of the organization unless it is a very small organization with little or no staff. Proponents of virtually all styles of board governance generally agree on one fundamental principle: boards and board members should not micromanage the affairs of the organization. The proper role of the board is "SOP." You may be familiar with that acronym when referring to "standard operating procedure." That acronym is also a useful reminder of the key areas of proper board involvement in a well-governed organization: Strategy, Oversight, and Policy.

Oversight, as contrasted with management, refers to the process of monitoring and evaluating the activities and operations of the organization. Logically then, financial oversight refers to the process of monitoring and evaluating the financial activities and operations of the organization.

The remainder of this book will concisely flesh out these concepts further, as we address the legal duties and responsibilities of the board, the board's use of finance and other committees, and the specific elements of effective financial oversight.

It is my sincere hope that you and your organization find the information in this book helpful. Helping organizations that make a positive and lasting difference in the lives of people is my calling...my life's work. I would welcome your comments on the book. You can email me directly at batts@nonprofitcpa.com.

May God bless you and your calling.

Mike Batts

1

THE DUTY OF BOARD MEMBERS TO OVERSEE FINANCIAL OPERATIONS

Good nonprofit organizations doing good work need good people to serve in the critically important role of governance.

This book is written with the assumption that your nonprofit organization is a corporation, which is the case for the vast majority of nonprofit organizations in the United States. The main principles would apply, however, to nonprofits organized as trusts or other less common forms of legal entities.

U.S. nonprofit corporations are legal entities formed pursuant to the laws of one of the states in the United States. Each state's laws contain specific statutes governing the activities of nonprofit (or "not-for-profit") corporations. The nonprofit corporation statutes of all states contain a roughly equivalent version of the following:

> All corporate powers must be exercised by or under the authority of, and the affairs of the corporation managed under the direction of, its board of directors, subject to any limitation set forth in the articles of incorporation. (Section 617.0801, Florida Statutes)

In other words, **the board of directors of a nonprofit corporation has full and final authority over the affairs of the organization**, unless the organization's articles of incorporation limit the board's authority in some way. (Such a limitation might exist, for example, when an organization has voting members and the articles of incorporation reserve for the membership the right to amend the articles of incorporation.)

Given this full and final authority over the affairs of an organization, the board is, then, ultimately responsible for overseeing and directing the activities of the organization. The board's authority and responsibility apply to *every* aspect of an organization's operations and activities. Of course, that includes financial operations and activities.

THE FIDUCIARY DUTY OF INDIVIDUAL BOARD MEMBERS

Board members each have a "fiduciary duty" with respect to overseeing the organization's activities. The fiduciary duty of a board member encompasses **the duty of care**, **the duty of loyalty**, and **the duty of obedience**.

THE DUTY OF CARE

The duty of care requires a board member to act in good faith, in a manner he or she reasonably believes to be in the best interests of the organization, and with the care an ordinarily prudent person would exercise in a like position under similar circumstances.

THE DUTY OF LOYALTY

The duty of loyalty requires a board member to act in the best interests of the organization rather than in his own interests or in the interests of his associates. For example, a board member who learns of a real estate investment opportunity during one of the nonprofit's board meetings may not seize the opportunity personally to the disadvantage of the organization. The duty of loyalty also requires the board member to avoid or fully disclose potential conflicts of interest by complying with the organization's conflicts-of-interest policy. (Policies are addressed in **Chapter 5** of this book.) It also encompasses maintaining appropriate confidentiality.

THE DUTY OF OBEDIENCE

The duty of obedience requires a board member to comply with applicable laws and to act in conformity with the organization's governing and policy documents.

FINANCIAL OVERSIGHT IS A VERY BIG PART OF *OVERALL* OVERSIGHT

Financial oversight is only one aspect of the board's duty to oversee all of the affairs of an organization...but it's a *big* one. The financial aspects of a nonprofit organization's activities are pervasive. The financial health of an organization directly impacts its ability to carry out its mission and purpose. Financial capacity directly impacts the extent to which an organization can engage in its key causes. And financial stewardship directly affects the viability and sustainability of an organization for the future.

Don't Worry, Be Prudent

The remainder of this chapter addresses risks that exist in the nonprofit sector. Don't allow this discussion of risk to intimidate you into not serving on the board or finance committee of a good nonprofit organization. The references to scandals and risks described in this chapter are intended to provide perspective as to why proper financial oversight is necessary and what can happen if it isn't exercised. In reality, the vast majority of nonprofit organizations have a strong desire to do the right things for the right reasons, while working to improve the lives of people. And significant scandals are, thankfully, a rarity. Good nonprofit organizations doing good work need good people to serve in the critically important role of governance. By maintaining an appropriate risk management strategy, the board can tremendously reduce the risk of unexpected liability for itself and for the organization.

Virtually All Risks Are Financial

Think of any recent high-profile scandal involving a nonprofit organization. Chances are that the scandal related primarily to financial matters...and if financial matters weren't at the center of the scandal, it is likely that they were still a significant aspect of the scandal. There is a scriptural principle that the love of money is the root of all kinds of evil. Similarly, mishandled financial matters are more often than not the root of nonprofit scandals. Misappropriation of assets, misdirection of donor-restricted contributions, excessive compensation, improper related party transactions, lavish or extravagant spending, violations of federal tax law, and improper private benefit are among the most common ways nonprofit scandals begin.

Financial improprieties like those listed in the preceding paragraph can have a *direct* financial impact on an organization. But virtually all operational risks have financial implications as well...potentially significant financial implications. For example, negligent or improper conduct by a nonprofit medical clinic's nurses can result in financial liability. The point is that virtually all of the risks faced by nonprofit organizations, including those that are not primarily financial in nature, have financial implications.

Reputational Risk – a Secondary Financial Risk

When high-profile adverse developments occur in an organization, the organization can sustain reputational damage. Donors may lose faith in the organization's credibility, board, and management...and they may stop or reduce their financial support of the organization as a result. So, an organization can not only find itself impacted directly by the financial implications of the actual underlying issue, it can be secondarily impacted financially by loss of trust on the part of donors and supporters.

ONE BIG PACKAGE

In fulfilling its duty to exercise effective financial oversight of a nonprofit organization, the board must realize that in addition to focusing specifically on direct financial matters, it must also address the financial implications of *all* areas of operations and risk. An organization can have the most well-groomed financial operations known to mankind, but if it is not properly screening child care workers, a seemingly nonfinancial operational issue can become a major financial, reputational, and personal tragedy. Effective financial oversight involves ensuring that the organization has a sound approach to overall risk management. In **Chapter 9** of this book, we address the topic of organization-wide risk management more thoroughly.

DEVOTING AMPLE TIME, RESOURCES, AND FOCUS TO FINANCIAL OVERSIGHT

Given the pervasive and critical significance of financial matters in a nonprofit organization, the board must ensure that it (the board) devotes ample time, resources, and focus to financial oversight of the organization. It can be tempting for a board to give short shrift to financial matters when board meeting agendas are heavy, everyone wants to limit meeting time, and board members are busy people. [By the way, you always want busy people on your board…successful and wise people are typically busy people…and people who are not busy are often more likely to make mountains out of mole hills.] The remainder of this book describes ways that the board can employ efficiencies in carrying out this responsibility, so we won't attempt to address those specific strategies here. But one element of the overall process *is* worth mentioning here. Having astute, capable, wise, respectful, conscientious, and highly responsive top management in the organization will have a dramatically favorable impact on the board's ability to devote ample time, resources, and focus to financial oversight.

A UNIQUE RESOURCE FOR YOU!

To help your board make sure your organization's financial oversight process is sound, this book contains an **Annual Financial Oversight Checklist for Boards and Finance Committees** that your board can use each year to address the topics described in every chapter of this book. See **Appendix A** for this special resource.

THE TONE AT THE TOP

Top management of a nonprofit organization <u>must</u> have a healthy regard for and focus on effective financial management of the organization. That includes making sure that all of the organization's financial bases are appropriately covered, and doing so in a manner that reflects the central importance of that responsibility. As stated in the introduction of this book, the board does not normally engage in financial *operations*, but it does engage in financial *oversight*. That oversight extends to making sure that top management properly carries out its duty to ensure healthy and effective financial operations.

Top management's effectiveness in this area begins with its perspective. Often referred to as the "tone at the top," we are talking here about the level of respect and focus that top management (particularly, the CEO or equivalent) pays to the area of proper and healthy financial operations. This is a key element of an organization's culture, and it has pervasive implications with respect to financial operations. If top management is capable and astute, and has a healthy regard for financial excellence, that will bode very well for an organization's financial (and other) operations, and it will make the board's job of financial oversight *much, much easier*. But if top management is incompetent in this area or has a low regard for financial administration, exhibited by traits like considering the accounting and financial operations to be a necessary evil, that organization is on a one-way bullet train to trouble... and the board's duty to exercise effective financial oversight will seem more like running a fire department. The board will be engaged in one emergency or challenge after another. That is, of course, assuming that the board itself is paying attention to these issues.

Is it true that top management is responsible for ensuring that an organization's financial operations are healthy and appropriate? Of course it is. But what happens when management carries out that responsibility poorly? We began this chapter by noting that the board has the ultimate legal responsibility for the activities of the organization. The board employs top management to direct the organization's operations and the board must ensure that management is appropriately accountable in carrying out that responsibility. Occasionally in practice, this author encounters a nonprofit organization in which the board considers itself as merely an advisory group for the CEO, and not the group ultimately responsible for the organization. That's not good.

If the tone at the top is not what it should be, the board should act. Sometimes, action by the board may include the necessity of replacing top management. If the board is unwilling (or for some reason unable) to act to remedy the situation, wise and capable people will not continue to serve on such a board.

BOARD MEMBER LIABILITY

Many urban legends and myths are propagated in nonprofit circles around the idea that nonprofit board members can easily be sued individually and held liable for their actions or inactions if they are not sufficiently careful in carrying out their duties.

It is true, of course, that anyone in America can sue anyone else in America for any reason any time, without regard to the merits of their case. Bearing the costs and possible repercussions of filing a baseless or frivolous lawsuit, however, is quite another matter, which is why such lawsuits are not common.

While it is certainly true that nonprofit organizations face exposure to a variety of risks and potential liability depending on the nature of their activities, it is actually quite rare for board members themselves to be sued in their individual capacities or held liable for damages in connection with their service on nonprofit boards.

CIVIL IMMUNITY

One major reason that nonprofit board members are rarely sued individually is that the laws of many states contain statutory provisions stating that volunteer board members (and often, other volunteers) of nonprofit organizations may not be held personally liable in connection with carrying out their duties in good faith. Obviously, a statutory "shield" of this type is a powerful force. Civil immunity laws generally will not, however, protect board members in cases of gross negligence, recklessness, or willful criminal conduct.

THE IMPORTANCE OF VOLUNTEERING VS. BEING COMPENSATED

A critical element of civil immunity laws is that they often apply only if the nonprofit board members are uncompensated. Very few nonprofit organizations compensate their board members for their service, as volunteer board service represents a charitable act in and of itself. For those organizations who would contemplate paying their board members, among the several considerations they should weigh is whether such compensation would cause the board members to lose statutory immunity from liability.

OTHER WAYS CIVIL IMMUNITY CAN BE LOST

Where state laws provide immunity for volunteer board members, such laws sometimes contain provisions stating that nonprofit board members lose their immunity if they engage in certain actions. For example, Florida law prohibits Florida nonprofit corporations from making loans to their officers or directors or to certain parties related to them. The law may be read to imply that violating the loan prohibition causes board members to lose the civil immunity that is otherwise available to them under the law.

Nonprofit boards should have their legal counsel advise them as to whether applicable state laws offer civil immunity for board members or other persons serving the organization. Counsel should also advise the board of any conditions for maintaining such immunity, so that the board may govern itself accordingly.

INDEMNIFICATION OF BOARD MEMBERS

Notwithstanding the fact that state law may provide some measure of immunity from liability for board members, nonprofit organizations commonly agree to indemnify (cover the cost of claims made against) their board members and officers in connection with carrying out their official duties. Organizations wishing to provide such indemnification typically include language to that effect in the organization's bylaws. As part of legal counsel's review of the bylaws, counsel should specifically address whether the indemnification language adequately and appropriately provides for the desired degree of protection.

DIRECTOR AND OFFICER LIABILITY INSURANCE

In addition to the layers of protection described previously in this chapter, nonprofit boards should insist that the organization maintain an insurance policy adequately covering the potential liability of board members in the event they are sued. As we recognized previously, anyone can sue anyone else any time for any reason, regardless of whether the case has merit. When faced with a lawsuit, board members must address not only the potential liability

> *Given the importance to the board members of such coverage, nonprofit organizations should make it a practice to provide board members with a copy of the D&O policy every year when it is renewed.*

of the claim itself, but also the legal costs of defending themselves. Board members need to know that not only has the organization agreed to indemnify them in such situations, but also that adequate funds are available to do so. That is the role of director and officer (D&O) liability insurance. The board should determine the level of coverage (coverage limits) that it considers adequate and select an insurance company (carrier) with a solid reputation and solid financial position. The board's legal counsel should review the insurance policy and advise the board regarding significant exclusions from coverage that may exist in the policy as well as other relevant aspects of the policy. Many persons knowledgeable about the world of nonprofit board service will refuse to serve on a board that does not have adequate D&O coverage. Given the importance to the board members of such coverage, nonprofit organizations should make it a practice to provide board members with a copy of the D&O policy every year when it is renewed, and the board's calendar should contain a reminder to do so each year.

2

THE FINANCE COMMITTEE

_____ - - _____

The finance committee is a board committee and it exists to help the board do its work.

COMMITTEES IN GENERAL

We established in Chapter 1 that the board of the organization has the ultimate legal authority and responsibility for *all* of the affairs of the organization – including financial activities. We also noted that financial oversight, while a very significant aspect of the board's overall duties, is just one aspect of the board's duty to oversee all of the affairs of the organization.

Given the multiple areas of responsibility and oversight that comprise the duties of nonprofit board members, some organizations utilize committees to help boards do their work. Let's take a brief look at the proper use and role of committees in general, and then we will address the specific utilization of a finance committee.

DO YOU NEED *ANY* COMMITTEES?

In speaking at various conferences and workshops nationally on nonprofit board governance topics, I have, on multiple occasions, asked participants, "What is your organization's basis for determining whether you need a board committee to address a specific area such as finance, human resources, or any other area?" I have yet to receive a clear and cohesive answer to the question. Boards often tend to create standing committees such as finance committees, audit committees, and development (fundraising) committees because they think it is just what nonprofits do...or because they know of other organizations that have them.

> *What is your organization's basis for determining whether you need a board committee?*

Before a board establishes a committee, it should have a conceptual framework for determining what committees are needed and the specific purpose for each committee. It is not appropriate to simply form a finance committee because the board thinks it is a good thing to do or because other similar organizations have one. Rather, the board should evaluate the nature of its activities and operations to determine if any committees are needed. If the board believes committees are needed, it should establish a framework of principles describing the conditions which should be present to justify formation of a particular committee.

The framework must keep in mind the fact that a board committee is not an operations group. Board committees exist to facilitate the work of the board, not the work of management, employees, or volunteers. For example, a group that engages in fundraising activities, public relations, or event planning is not (or should not be) a board committee. Such a group is an operating or activity group that should operate under the authority of the CEO and management. Since boards should limit their activities to the areas of strategy, oversight, and policy (as described in this book's **Introduction**), the same should be true of the board's committees; otherwise they will be dysfunctional.

APPLYING A ZERO-BASED APPROACH

Many organizations do not need board committees of any type. Depending on the performance and approach of top management and the nature and scope of the organization's activities, a board may be able to operate perfectly well with no committees. Nonprofit organizations should take a zero-based approach to establishing committees – that is, starting with the premise that *no* board committees are to be utilized unless the need is clearly identified and justified.

In rare cases, a specific type of committee may be required by state law. (For example, the laws of California require an audit committee for certain types of nonprofit organizations of a certain size.)

STANDING VS. AD HOC COMMITTEES

A board committee is either a standing committee or an ad hoc (temporary, as needed) committee. Ad hoc committees can be very useful to assist the board in evaluating a proposed strategy or policy issue that involves significant detail. Rather than attempt to have the entire board address the matter in detail, with drafts and redrafts, the board may create an ad hoc committee to perform the detailed work and provide a recommendation to the full board. If the board creates an ad hoc committee for such a purpose, the committee should have a clear charter and should be disbanded when its work is complete.

CRITERIA FOR ESTABLISHING A BOARD COMMITTEE

Every organization is unique and there is no one-size-fits-all set of principles for determining whether an organization should have board committees. There are, however, common considerations in making such a determination. These considerations include:

- **Whether the board can devote sufficient time in board meetings to exercise appropriate oversight.** Given the comprehensive nature of the board's responsibilities for an organization, it is important that the board be able to devote adequate time to its oversight of the organization overall. The board should meet frequently enough and long enough to accomplish that objective. A number of variables affect a board's capacity in this regard. Factors having the most significant impact include the capabilities of top management and the nature and extent of management's reporting to the board. A reporting model in which management provides clear, concise, and thorough reports with respect to all key areas of operations will favorably impact the efficiency and capacity of the board overall. This book addresses reporting and monitoring in more detail in **Chapter 6**. If the board does not have adequate time in its board meetings to appropriately exercise its oversight responsibility in a key area, that area may be a candidate for utilization of a board committee.

- **Whether board members and others are willing to spend time outside of board meetings and attend separate committee meetings.** One of the most significant disadvantages of establishing any committee is the additional time commitment involved on the part of committee members. Participation on a committee requires additional meetings and the between-meeting preparation that goes with them. A factor affecting a person's willingness to serve on a nonprofit board is the time commitment such service entails. Committees may be composed entirely or partially of board members, but every board committee must have board member representation. Requiring board members to serve on one or more committees expands that person's required time commitment and may adversely affect his/her willingness to serve the organization at all.

- **The nature, size, scope, complexity, and risk of the organization's activities.** The larger, more complex, and more high-risk an organization's activities, the more likely it is that one or more board committees may be helpful.

- **The pervasiveness of a particular area of board oversight.** Areas of board oversight that are particularly pervasive or complex may warrant utilization of a committee to assist the board in doing its work. For example, financial matters are typically pervasive in any organization – and the complexity of the organization's financial activities should be considered. Overall risk management may also be considered a pervasive area for oversight, depending on the facts. Each organization should evaluate its activities in assessing the pervasiveness and complexity of a particular area.

- **Whether members of the board have the expertise to appropriately monitor and evaluate a particular area of oversight.** Boards composed of members with little financial expertise are more likely to benefit from (and even need) the assistance of a finance committee. (It is not a good idea for a board not to have some members with strong financial expertise.) Organizations that conduct high-risk activities (e.g., counseling, health care services, child care, etc.) should determine if the organization's board members have the expertise to evaluate the programs and related risks associated with those activities. For example, if an organization provides health care services, it is necessary for the board to have the ability to monitor and evaluate the conduct of and risks associated with those services. Ordinarily, that would entail having one or more health care professionals on the board or having a risk management committee (or other appropriate oversight committee) that includes such individuals.

COMMITTEE CHARTERS

No board should have any committee without a very clear charter setting forth the purpose, authority, composition, and objectives of the committee. Without a clear charter, board committees will likely have a difficult time discerning whether an issue or a decision is within the scope of their responsibility or authority. Such confusion will likely lead to dysfunctional board governance. A committee charter should be approved by the full board.

COMMITTEE AUTHORITY

Board committees are rarely vested with authority to act on behalf of the full board. Much more commonly, a board committee addresses specific board-level issues in more detail than the full board wishes to do itself and then makes recommendations to the full board.

THE FINANCE COMMITTEE CHARTER

We'll assume at this point that your board has determined, taking into consideration appropriate factors like those described above, that it could possibly benefit from the utilization of a finance committee. The next step is to define clearly the **purpose** and **authority** of the finance committee, along with its **composition**.

PURPOSE AND AUTHORITY CONSIDERATIONS

In defining the purpose and authority of the finance committee, nonprofit boards often delegate to the committee the responsibility of assisting the board in carrying out its duty to exercise financial oversight of the organization. While some organizations vest their finance committees with authority to make final decisions on behalf of the board, granting such authority to a finance committee is rare. In most cases, the board charges the finance committee with performing monitoring, analysis, and evaluation of financial matters on behalf of the board and making specific recommendations to the board for action. A hybrid approach is also possible and somewhat common. In a hybrid approach to granting committee authority, a board will typically limit the ability of the committee to act on behalf of the board to only those matters for which the board specifically delegates such authority...with the board retaining the authority to act with respect to all other matters. An example of application of hybrid authority granted to a finance committee would be where the board approves the organization's annual budget, retains the right to approve variances from the budget in excess of a particular threshold, and grants to the finance committee the authority to approve variances below the board-retained threshold.

STICKING TO BOARD-LEVEL WORK

Both the board and the finance committee must keep in mind that the finance committee is a *board* committee and it exists to help the board do its work. Just like the board itself, the finance committee's purview should be in the areas of SOP – *strategy, oversight, and policy*, and the finance committee should not attempt to intervene in operations...including financial operations.

What does that mean practically? It means that the finance committee should engage itself in matters such as evaluation of proposed budgets for recommendations to the board, addressing long-term financial strategies, assessment of the organization's financial health and financial practices, monitoring of the organization's financial activities, approving financial policies and policy modifications for recommendation to the board, and other similar matters. The finance committee **is not** a substitute for a chief financial officer (CFO) or for any other member of management, and the finance committee should ordinarily not be making decisions regarding operating matters. This is sometimes an area in which organizations struggle, because it can be tempting for members of a finance committee to immerse themselves in the details of a particular issue. If members of the finance committee have financial expertise, the temptation can be even greater.

Why avoid intervening in operating matters? Because when a board or board committee makes operating decisions or takes operating actions, it undermines the role and authority of management, and no great members of management will stick around in an organization where their role and authority are undermined. In a well-governed organization, the board hires the president/CEO of the organization and the president/CEO is the board's sole direct report. Other members of management, such as the Chief Financial Officer or equivalent, report to and are subordinate to the president/CEO. The president/CEO is charged with leading and running the operations of the organization within a framework of mission, purpose, strategy, policy, and budgeting established by the board. The CFO reports directly to the CEO – not to the board and not to the finance committee.

AN EXAMPLE OF MEDDLING IN OPERATIONS

Let's consider an example. The CEO and CFO of Help Everyone Charity decide that the organization needs to upgrade its donor relations and contributions management software. The CEO authorizes the CFO to evaluate options and make a decision about which software application to purchase. Adequate funds are budgeted in the capital expenditures and operating budgets to cover the cost of the software upgrade, which is going to be rather expensive. The CFO evaluates options and has determined after extensive research that a particular application is the best fit for the organization. It will cost $150,000. During a regular finance committee meeting, the finance committee learns of the planned software purchase and one of the finance committee members asks the CFO if there were less expensive options available and asks the CFO to describe the process used to make the decision – a fair question. The CFO advises the committee that there are, indeed, alternatives priced significantly lower but that they do not have features that management considers essential, and they were, therefore, excluded from further consideration. The finance committee expresses concern about the cost difference and then votes to require the CFO to bring all the relevant information to the finance committee for the finance committee to evaluate the options. The CFO does as instructed and the finance committee directs the CFO to choose a less costly software alternative.

The example described in the preceding paragraph is not far-fetched. Such incidents occur in board rooms and finance committee meetings across the country all the time. When they do, the board or committee often doesn't stop to realize how much damage it has done to the role and authority of management. In the example above, the finance committee has not only undermined the authority of the CFO, it has also undermined the authority of the CEO. The CEO authorized the CFO to make the decision. The funds were budgeted. And then the finance committee stepped in and took over. In addition to offending the members of top management by meddling in operations in this manner, such meddling also breeds insecurity on the part of management. If the board or finance committee has a tendency to meddle in or second-guess management's operating decisions, how can management know that *any* of its decisions will be respected? Capable members of management will not stay long in an organization in which the board or its committees second-guess or meddle in management's operating decisions.

IS IT EVER OK FOR THE BOARD OR FINANCE COMMITTEE TO ENGAGE IN OPERATING MATTERS?

Notwithstanding the principles described previously in this chapter regarding the proper role of the board and finance committee in a well-governed organization, there may be occasions when it is appropriate for the board or one of its committees to intervene in operating matters. When an organization makes a pervasively significant financial decision, such as entering into a large new loan, it is appropriate for the board (and, if applicable, the finance committee) to evaluate the nature, terms, and advisability of the arrangement – since it is pervasively significant to the organization overall. Arguably, such a decision is as much a strategy decision as it is an operating decision.

Another scenario in which the board or finance committee *needs* to intervene is failure on the part of management to act appropriately or responsibly.

EXAMPLE OF NECESSARY BOARD OR FINANCE COMMITTEE INTERVENTION

A nonprofit organization has a conflicts-of-interest policy which states that its board members and top officers must submit any proposed business transaction to the finance committee and board for preapproval if a related party (a board member, a member of top management, a member of their families, or one of their businesses) has a financial interest in the transaction. The organization learns that its CEO has caused the organization to enter into a very large vendor service agreement with a company owned by his brother and the CEO did not present the arrangement for preapproval as required by the conflicts-of-interest policy. The board meets and determines that the action was inappropriate, determines that the business arrangement was not in the best interests of the organization, and that the CEO had knowingly violated the organization's policy. The board then takes action to terminate the CEO and CFO (who did not protest the arrangement) and directs the finance committee to terminate the business arrangement and enter into a new one with an unrelated party.

A scenario like that described in the preceding paragraph is dire and, thankfully, very rare. It is provided as an extreme example of a situation in which there may be a compelling reason for the board or its committees to intervene in operating matters.

COMPOSITION OF THE FINANCE COMMITTEE

If the organization has a finance committee, it should be composed of members who have financial and business expertise. Given the role and purpose of the finance committee, it would be of little value to fill it with people who do not have skills in the financial arena. Ideally, the finance committee members would draw from a variety of business backgrounds and professions, including general business leaders, accountants, bankers, investment professionals, and other financially savvy leaders who have a passion for the mission and work of the organization.

REFERENCES TO A FINANCE COMMITTEE IN THIS BOOK

Given the fact that an organization may decide, as described in this chapter, not to utilize a finance committee or its equivalent – and the reality that even if a finance committee is utilized, the governing body (board) of the organization is ultimately responsible for the affairs of the organization – the remainder of this book generally refers to the board when referring to the financial oversight body. The fact that it does so is not intended to imply that a finance committee is not necessary or helpful for any particular organization. Rather, reference to the board is a practical means of simplifying the text for the reader.

SAMPLE FINANCE COMMITTEE CHARTER

[This is a sample charter with sample provisions. The content of this sample charter is not intended to imply that any particular provision herein is necessary or appropriate for a particular organization, nor is it the intent of the author to imply that all of the provisions of this sample charter represent best practices for nonprofit organizations. The board of each organization with a finance committee should establish a charter for the committee with specific provisions that are uniquely appropriate for the organization.]

COMMITTEE PURPOSE AND RESPONSIBILITIES

The Finance Committee assists the board in fulfilling its financial oversight responsibilities. As a standing committee of the board, the Finance Committee:

1. Approves and recommends to the board for approval the annual operating, capital expenditure, debt reduction, and restricted gift spending budgets prepared by staff;

2. Approves and recommends to the board for approval policies and policy modifications involving financial matters for the organization as deemed appropriate;

3. Reviews and evaluates internal and external financial reports (including the annual Form 990, if applicable) provided by the staff;

4. Regularly monitors and evaluates the financial activities and financial condition of the organization;

5. Annually communicates with the independent auditing firm (unless the board appoints a separate audit committee tasked with that responsibility) to receive and evaluate the results of the annual audit of the organization's financial statements, together with reports by the auditing firm on internal control and other matters;

6. Ensures that the organization maintains an adequate organization-wide risk management plan and strategy to protect the organization financially – such plan and strategy to incorporate considerations of operating risks, compliance with applicable laws, and other appropriate risk management practices;

7. Ensures that the board of directors is appropriately and timely apprised of the committee's work and of financial matters related to the organization; and

8. Engages in any other activities necessary to effectively oversee the financial operations of the organization.

AUTHORITY OF THE COMMITTEE

The committee has such authority as is set forth in the bylaws of the organization. The committee is authorized to make recommendations to the board for action by the board. Unless empowered by the bylaws or by specific action of the board of directors, the committee is not empowered to act on behalf of the board or the corporation.

COMMITTEE MEETINGS

The committee shall meet at such times as are set forth in the bylaws or, subject to provisions in the bylaws, on the call of the committee chairman at times and locations established by the committee chairman.

The organization's CEO and CFO shall attend meetings of the committee except during executive sessions (sessions in which employees of the organization are excused).

ACTIONS OF THE COMMITTEE

A quorum of the committee members shall exist at any properly called meeting if a majority of the members of the committee are present. Actions or decisions of the committee are made by a majority vote of the members present at a properly called meeting at which a quorum is established.

COMMITTEE COMPOSITION

The corporate Treasurer of the organization shall serve as a voting member of the committee *ex officio*, and shall be the chairman of the committee. As provided in the organization's bylaws, the chairman of the board appoints other members to the committee for one-year terms. The committee shall consist of at least five members and no more than seven members, which number includes the Treasurer. In addition to the Treasurer, at least one other member of the committee shall be a member of the board of directors. The chairman of the board should seek to include as members of the committee people who possess excellent skills in the disciplines of accounting, finance, and business practices. Additionally, in order to maintain stability in the composition of the committee, the chairman of the board should generally strive to avoid a change of more than two members of the committee from one year to the next unless a compelling reason exists for a greater degree of transition.

MODIFICATIONS TO THIS CHARTER

This charter is to be modified as deemed appropriate by the board of directors of the organization. The finance committee may recommend modifications to the board for approval.

3

Audits and Other Accountability Practices

————————— - - —————————

A well-performed audit should yield significant value.

*Given the fact that an organization may decide, as described in **Chapter 2**, not to utilize a finance committee or its equivalent – and the reality that even if a finance committee is utilized, the governing body (board) of the organization is ultimately responsible for the affairs of the organization – this book generally refers to the board when referring to the financial oversight body. The fact that it does so is not intended to imply that a finance committee is not necessary or helpful for any particular organization. Rather, reference to the board is a practical means of simplifying the text for the reader.*

Use of the Term "Audit" in This Book

The term "audit" can and does mean many different things to different people in different contexts. A common theme among practical definitions is that an audit is an "examination" process designed to address validity, reliability, accuracy, and accountability. Since this book addresses the topic of financial oversight, we will be addressing audits and other accountability practices primarily as they relate to financial activities. In this book, the term "audit" and references to other accountability activities are used to refer to activities conducted or contracted by an organization for the purposes of addressing:

- The reliability of financial statements or reports;

- Whether the organization has vulnerabilities in internal controls, tax compliance, or legal matters; and

- Whether certain aspects of an organization's operations are being carried out as intended or expected.

EXTERNAL AND INTERNAL AUDITS

Audits and other financial accountability activities are conducted by parties who are either external or internal to the organization. Nonprofit organizations tend to utilize internal and external audits and other accountability practices in ways that correlate to the size of the organization. Smaller organizations tend to utilize internal accountability processes that are typically performed by members of the organization's governing body, by its finance committee or equivalent, or by volunteer supporters of the organization. In smaller organizations, the procedures tend to be less formal. Larger organizations find it more difficult for board members, committee members, or volunteers to adequately perform all of the internal accountability functions needed. Accordingly, larger nonprofit organizations (often, those with annual revenues exceeding $2 million) commonly engage external auditors. Very large nonprofit organizations (typically, those with annual revenues in the tens or hundreds of millions of dollars) sometimes engage external auditors in addition to maintaining a regular, formal internal audit function – often involving the employment of an internal auditor on staff or contracting with a vendor for formal internal audit services.

> *Nonprofit organizations tend to utilize internal and external audits and other accountability practices in ways that correlate to the size of the organization.*

EXTERNAL AUDITS AND OTHER CPA-PERFORMED ENGAGEMENTS

Nonprofit organizations have external audits or other accountability-oriented services performed by certified public accounting firms for a variety of reasons. Sometimes, lending institutions require an organization to have an external audit of its financial statements as a condition of making a loan to the organization. Some organizations seek grants from foundations or other funders who require audited financial statements as a condition of making a grant. These and other externally-imposed requirements for an organization to have an external audit do not, however, represent the highest and best reasons for an organization to have an external audit. An organization that has an external audit performed solely for the purpose of complying with a contractual or funding obligation typically sees little value in the audit beyond that of meeting the organization's obligations. Organization leaders who view audits in this way may have little interest in the quality of the audit firm utilized to perform the engagement and may have little interest in the value that an excellent external audit can provide to an organization.

The highest and best reason for an organization to have an external audit is to facilitate the organization's financial integrity and accountability and to increase the likelihood that significant internal control deficiencies, tax compliance vulnerabilities, or similar matters will come to the attention of the organization's leadership before they become real problems for the organization.

Certified Public Accountants (CPAs) and CPA firms are uniquely licensed as a matter of state law to perform audits and provide certain other services with respect to an organization's financial statements. It is a violation of state law for anyone other than a CPA or a CPA firm to hold himself, herself, or itself out as providing audit, assurance, or attestation with respect to an organization's financial statements. Organizations should be careful when seeking an external audit to ensure that the person or firm being engaged is licensed or legally authorized to practice as a CPA or CPA firm. Some non-CPA individuals and companies hold themselves out in a manner that implies that they perform external audits or similar services. Nonprofit organizations should avoid such practitioners.

The highest quality external audits for nonprofit organizations are those provided by independent CPA firms with extensive and reputable experience serving nonprofit organizations. Firms with such experience should be able to help the organization proactively identify issues that warrant attention.

Is an Audit Committee Necessary?

Some nonprofits choose to form and utilize an audit committee to oversee the audit process. As described in detail in **Chapter 2**, the decision as to whether to utilize a committee of *any* type should be based on specific parameters and considerations. Except in rare cases (e.g., California law governing certain nonprofit organizations), a nonprofit organization is not required as a matter of law to have an audit committee. Even if an organization does have an audit committee, the committee is still performing the work of the board under the authority of the board...and the entire board should be fully apprised of the work of the audit committee. Most nonprofit organizations can function quite adequately without an audit committee, with the board directly overseeing the audit process. After all, the board should be fully aware of the results of the audit process regardless.

What about Having the Finance Committee Oversee the Audit Process?

If your organization utilizes a finance committee (see **Chapter 2**), a natural question would be whether the finance committee should perform the role of overseeing the audit process on behalf of the board. Some people take the position that an organization's audit committee should be separate from its finance committee since the finance committee oversees financial operations. Given the practical implications of separating the committees, many nonprofit organizations that utilize finance committees have them serve in the capacity of the audit committee, or they utilize a subcommittee of the finance committee to do so.

ELEMENTS OF AUDIT OVERSIGHT

Whether the board oversees the audit process directly or through the use of a committee, certain elements of the process of should be present.

- The board or committee should be composed of at least some members who have financial and business experience and knowledge sufficient to permit them to perform the duties well.

- The board or board-authorized committee should engage the independent CPA firm directly, and establish lines of reporting and communication making it clear that the CPA firm reports directly to the board or committee for the audit process, and not to management.

- The board or committee should evaluate the quality and performance of the independent CPA firm and, to the best of its reasonable ability, determine that the firm is independent with respect to the organization, that it is well-experienced in serving organizations like theirs, and that it performs the work professionally.

- The board or committee should have a clear understanding of the scope of the audit or other engagement, the work to be performed, and the reports to be issued.

- The board or committee should evaluate the audit reports and findings and ensure that appropriate action or follow-up is pursued for any matters identified by the auditor as warranting attention.

- If the audit oversight process is performed by a committee, the committee most definitely should ensure that the entire board is fully apprised of the results of the audit process, including any findings or recommendations by the auditor that may be relevant to the board in ensuring that its financial oversight duty is properly carried out.

- If the organization utilizes an audit committee, the committee should have a charter outlining the purpose and duties of the committee as described above.

In addition to independent external audits, CPA firms offer other levels of service with respect to an organization's financial statements and/ or operating activities. Following is a description of the primary levels of engagement available from CPA firms, along with commentary regarding the relative value and usefulness of each.

AUDIT

An audit is the highest level of assurance a CPA firm can provide with respect to an organization's financial statements. An audit provides the organization's governing body with the auditor's opinion as to whether the financial statements are presented fairly, in all material respects, in conformity with the method of accounting utilized. The opinion offers reasonable, but not absolute, assurance with respect to the financial statements to which it applies.

In performing an audit, the CPA firm should obtain an understanding of the organization's internal control and assess fraud risk as it relates to the financial statements. The firm should also corroborate the amounts and disclosures included in the financial statements by obtaining audit evidence through inquiry, physical inspection, observation, third-party confirmations, examination, analytical procedures, and other procedures.

A properly performed audit should result in the following reports, at a minimum:

- An opinion on the financial statements

- Financial statements and related disclosures

- A report addressing any material weaknesses or significant deficiencies in internal control identified by the CPA firm in performing the engagement

   [Note – some CPA firms do not issue a report in connection with audits in which the CPA does not identify any material weaknesses or significant deficiencies in internal control. Professional auditing standards, however, permit an auditor to issue a report stating that he/she did not identify any material weaknesses in internal control. The author recommends that an organization request its auditor to

issue a report addressing internal control regardless of whether the auditor identifies material weaknesses or significant deficiencies in the course of the audit.]

- A report to those charged with governance oversight of the organization regarding certain matters related to the audit process itself (e.g., independence of the auditors, sensitive items in the financial statements, difficulties performing the engagement, etc.).

COMMENTARY

A well-performed audit conducted by a CPA firm with extensive reputable experience serving nonprofit organizations should yield significant value to an organization and its leaders. An audit results in an opinion on the financial statements by the CPA, providing reasonable assurance that the financial statements are fairly stated (assuming the audit test work supports such a conclusion). No other level of engagement provides a comparable level of assurance regarding the organization's financial statements. The other levels of engagement described below are substantially less in scope than an audit.

Additionally, in an audit, the CPA is required to obtain an understanding of the organization's internal control and assess the risk of material misstatements, including the risk of fraud, in the financial statements to the extent necessary to perform the audit. In the event that the auditor identifies fraud, material weaknesses, or significant deficiencies in the organization's internal control, the auditor is required to report such matters to the organization's leadership. The auditor's report addressing internal control can be one of the most valuable products of the independent external audit process. A well-performed audit that identifies weaknesses in an organization's internal controls can help the organization improve its systems, processes, and protocols to reduce the risk of improprieties and financial misstatements in the future.

Finally, if the CPA firm performing the audit has extensive experience addressing tax and operational matters for nonprofit organizations, the CPA firm may utilize the audit process to identify other vulnerabilities such as tax compliance risks or opportunities such as tax exemptions not fully utilized by the organization. When a firm provides such value-added commentary to an organization for which it is performing an audit, the overall value received by the organization in an audit process is enhanced further.

While an independent external audit provides the most value to the organization of all of the types of engagements a CPA firm may provide, an audit is also typically the most costly type of engagement. Accordingly, nonprofit organizations considering having an independent external audit must weigh the value of the services to be received with the overall cost. For this reason, it is more common for larger nonprofit organizations (typically, those with annual revenues of $2 million or more) to have independent external audits than it is for smaller organizations to do so.

REVIEW

A review of financial statements provides the organization's governing body with comfort that, based on the CPA's review, the CPA is not aware of any material modifications that should be made to the financial statements for the statements to be in conformity with the method of accounting utilized. A review is substantially less in scope than an audit, and does not require obtaining an understanding of internal control, assessing the risk of fraud, or testing the organization's records.

In a review engagement, the CPA firm performs procedures (primarily analytical procedures and inquiries) that will provide a reasonable basis for obtaining limited assurance that there are no material modifications that should be made to the financial statements.

A properly performed review should result in the following reports:

- A review report expressing limited assurance on the financial statements

- Financial statements and related disclosures

Note that a review does not result in a report addressing the organization's internal control, since a CPA firm performing a review is not required to obtain an understanding of the organization's internal control as part of conducting the engagement.

COMMENTARY

In the opinion of the author, a review of an organization's financial statements has limited value, and is often obtained by an organization in scenarios where the organization is contractually required to obtain a review or an audit of its financial statements and the organization does not wish to incur the cost of an audit. A review provides the organization's governing body with "limited assurance" regarding the reliability of the financial statements. The CPA firm conducting a review is not required to obtain an understanding of the organization's internal control, nor is the CPA firm required to perform any specific tests of the underlying documentation supporting the organization's financial statements. As a result, a review engagement typically does not involve any report to the organization with respect to its internal control, tax compliance matters, or other potential operational risks or vulnerabilities. If an organization wishes to engage a CPA firm for the purpose of obtaining assurance with respect to the financial statements and to obtain information about weaknesses in the organization's internal control, a review engagement is not adequate for such purposes. An organization should carefully evaluate the value being received before entering into an engagement to have a review of its financial statements.

COMPILATION

A compilation represents the most basic level of service a CPA firm may provide in which a report is issued with respect to an organization's financial statements. In a compilation engagement, the CPA assists management in presenting financial information in the form of financial statements without undertaking to obtain or provide any assurance with respect to the financial statements. In a compilation, the CPA firm is required to have an understanding of the industry in which the client operates, obtain knowledge about the client, read the financial statements, and consider whether the financial statements appear appropriate in form and free from obvious material errors.

A compilation does not contemplate performing inquiry, analytical procedures, or other procedures ordinarily performed in a review; or obtaining an understanding of the organization's internal control, assessing fraud risk, or testing of accounting records – elements of an audit. Compiled financial statements may be prepared without disclosures (notes to the financial statements). The compilation report provides no assurance whatsoever with respect to the financial statements.

A properly performed compilation typically results in the following reports:

- A compilation report expressing no assurance on the financial statements

- Financial statements and (if applicable) related disclosures

COMMENTARY

A compilation is the simplest and lowest cost engagement option involving an organization's financial statements in which a report is issued by a CPA firm. A compilation is often vernacularly described within the accounting profession as "taking the client's financial information, without checking or testing it, and putting it into the format of proper financial statements." That description, while simple, does reasonably sum up the nature of a compilation engagement. Typically, the CPA firm assists the organization in preparing financial statements in the format required for the particular method of accounting used. The CPA firm uses the organization's financial information to do so, but the firm does not test the information as it would in an audit, nor does it perform analytical procedures and inquiries as it would in a review. While it is true that a compilation results in a report from the CPA, the report specifically states that the CPA provides no assurance with respect to the financial statements.

There are multiple reasons that nonprofit organizations may engage CPA firms to perform compilations of their financial statements. In many cases, the reason revolves around the lack of ability or capacity of the organization's staff to prepare proper financial statements in conformity with an applicable method of accounting. By engaging a CPA firm to perform a compilation, the organization essentially contracts with the CPA firm to prepare the organization's financial statements in a proper format. The compiled financial statements may be used for internal purposes. Sometimes, a compilation of the organization's financial statements is obtained in response to a requirement by the organization's lender as a condition of making a loan to the organization. (A compilation may be an acceptable level of financial statement engagement for a lender when the loan amount is small. Typically, the larger the loan amount, the higher the level of financial statement engagement a lender may require.)

Given the fact that a CPA firm provides no assurance with respect to the financial statements in a compilation engagement, an organization should not expect or depend on a compilation engagement to address the reliability or accuracy of the organization's financial statements. The organization also should not have the impression that a compilation engagement will help the organization identify any internal control deficiencies that may exist, tax compliance risks that may exist, or other vulnerabilities. While a compilation may serve a useful purpose such as one or more of those described above, its value is severely limited – a fact which nonprofit organizations should take into consideration when considering such an engagement.

OUTSOURCED ACCOUNTING SERVICES (WITH OR WITHOUT COMPILATION)

A nonprofit organization may also outsource its accounting and financial reporting processes to an accounting firm. In outsourced accounting arrangements, the accounting firm takes on the role that would normally be performed by the organization's internal accounting staff. Various service providers offer various forms of outsourced accounting. Historically, outsourced accounting services tended to be in the form of after-the-fact bookkeeping services. In recent years, some accounting firms have begun to offer live or real-time outsourced accounting services in which the accounting firm takes on the role of day-to-day processing of transactions and accounting records. Depending on state law, it may be possible for some service providers that are not CPA firms to provide certain outsourced accounting services. In some states, such services may not be referred to as "accounting" services unless they are provided by a CPA firm. Nonprofit organizations interested in engaging a firm other than a CPA firm to provide outsourced accounting services should ensure that the firm is properly licensed to provide the required services.

If outsourced accounting services are provided by a CPA firm, such services may (by mutual agreement of the organization and the CPA firm) include the production of financial statements with a compilation report by the CPA firm. Depending on the nature of the services provided by the CPA firm, the CPA firm may not be independent with respect to the organization's financial statements. Professional standards governing the accounting profession permit a CPA firm to issue a compilation report with respect to an organization's financial statements even if the CPA firm is not independent with respect to the organization. In such cases, the lack of independence must be disclosed in the compilation report.

COMMENTARY

Nonprofit organizations wishing to simplify their internal responsibilities for financial administration may find that outsourcing the accounting function to a CPA firm or other service provider allows the organization's leaders to focus more on mission and program-related activities and less on administrative matters. In some cases, the cost of such an arrangement may be less than if the organization were to perform the services internally. If an organization does outsource its accounting and internal financial reporting responsibilities and can also benefit from a compilation report on its financial statements, the organization can engage a CPA firm to perform the outsourced services and include a compilation of the appropriate financial statements. Such an arrangement may be appropriate in cases where a lender or other third party requires compiled financial statements.

AGREED-UPON PROCEDURES

Another type of engagement for which an organization may involve a CPA firm is an agreed-upon procedures engagement. As the term implies, an agreed-upon procedures engagement is an engagement in which the CPA performs certain procedures which have been agreed-upon by the client in an agreement that specifically describes the procedures to be performed. An organization may engage a CPA to perform procedures that are important to the organization for some reason or that help the organization assess its practices in certain areas. Professional standards provide significant freedom for the CPA in designing an agreed-upon procedures engagement.

The CPA firm performing the agreed-upon procedures will provide a report of the results of the procedures performed. Professional standards governing the accounting profession provide, however, that the reported results are to represent the objective outcomes of the procedures performed. The CPA firm does not provide an opinion regarding the procedures performed or regarding the items or matters that are subjected to the procedures. For example, it would be inappropriate under professional standards for a CPA to include in an agreed-upon procedures report language such as, "therefore, we believe the cash balance as of December 31 is reasonable," or "accordingly, the procedures related to reconciling contributions revenue are being correctly followed by the organization's staff." An example of appropriate language in an agreed-upon procedures report related to year-end cash balances follows:

> We inspected the original bank statement as of December 31, 20XX, and compared the ending balance per the bank statement to the balance per bank on the organization's bank reconciliation report as of the same date without exception. We identified deposits in transit on the organization's bank reconciliation as of December 31 individually in excess of $1,000, and traced the items to the organization's original January bank statement, noting that all items cleared the bank within the first five days of January without exception. Further, we identified debits to the organization's bank account as reported in the first 10 days of January on the organization's original January bank statement, and traced those in excess of $500 to the organization's December 31 reconciliation report, without exception.
>
> *[Note that the language in the example provided above does not include qualitative assessments with respect to the procedures*

performed. For example, the CPA does not use the words "reasonable" or "opinion" in this language. He merely describes the procedures performed and objectively states that they were performed "without exception." Had there been exceptions, the CPA would specifically describe the exceptions noted. An agreed-upon procedures engagement does not result in an assessment of the quality of an item nor an opinion with respect to it.]

Following are examples of procedures that an organization may agree with a CPA firm to perform in connection with the organization's financial operations. [Note that these are merely a couple of examples. The organization and the CPA may agree to a variety of procedures provided that they can be performed objectively and reported on objectively. Specific dates and other parameters, or their basis of selection must be described in order for the CPA to perform the procedures objectively.]

- Compare the cash balance per bank as reported in the original bank statement to the balance used by the organization in performing its year-end bank account reconciliation. Trace deposits in transit reported on the organization's bank account reconciliation in excess of a certain amount to clearing the bank within a certain number of days as noted on the original bank statement for the following month. Trace debits clearing in the original bank statement for the first 10 days of the following month to the outstanding debits reported by the organization in its year end bank reconciliation report. Describe any exceptions that are identified.

- For three separate months haphazardly selected by the CPA, compare the amounts recognized as contribution revenue in the organization's general ledger with the amounts included in the organization's donor contribution database for the same period. Identify the reason and basis provided by the organization's staff for any difference in excess of $1,000 for a particular month and report same.

COMMENTARY

Given the constraints that apply to an agreed-upon procedures engagement under the professional standards that govern the accounting profession, the process of planning and specifically tailoring an agreed-upon procedures engagement to meet the particular needs of an organization can be intricate and tedious. Further, since an agreed-upon procedures engagement results in an objective report describing the specific outcomes of the procedures and not an opinion or other qualitative assessment, the report may have limited value for the organization. An agreed-upon procedures engagement does not provide assurance regarding the items tested, nor does it involve making corrections to the organization's accounting records or financial statements.

Agreed-upon procedures engagements may be useful when an organization has certain elements or practices for which it wishes to have independently performed procedures to address or test. In reality, such situations are rare.

Nonprofit organizations should also be careful when considering an agreed-upon procedures engagement to address whether the CPA firm has the experience necessary to plan and perform the engagement properly. For example, while the professional standards prohibit a CPA firm from making qualitative statements or providing an opinion with respect to procedures performed in an agreed-upon procedures engagement, some CPA firms unwittingly violate the standards and issue reports using terms such as "reasonable," "in our opinion," or other similar verbiage.

ADVISORY SERVICES

In addition to the various levels of service described above for which an organization may engage an accounting firm, an organization may also consider engaging a firm to provide advisory services with respect to certain aspects of its financial operations. Advisory services engagements provided by CPA firms may take many forms, but they generally involve an agreement to provide professional advice or recommendations to the organization with respect to a particular area of the organization's financial operations. Examples of areas for which the organization may wish to engage a CPA firm to provide advisory services include, but are not limited to, the following:

- Internal control matters;

- Tax compliance matters;

- Efficiencies in financial operations;

- Accounting treatment for certain transaction types;

- Business-oriented commentary on proposed transactions;

- Risk management; and

- Board governance.

COMMENTARY

A good, regular, and proactive working relationship with a CPA firm can be a great source of help to organization leaders as they address business, financial, risk, and operational matters. Such working relationships are common among larger nonprofit organizations that use their professional advisors as sounding boards in a proactive manner to facilitate and reduce the risk associated with significant new transactions, initiatives, and policy matters.

INTERNAL AUDITS

Internal audits and similar activities may be conducted in a variety of ways. In some cases, an organization's board members or finance committee members or equivalent perform the tasks. In other cases, volunteer supporters of the organization perform the duties. In larger settings, the organization may contract an individual or a firm to perform procedures and in very large organizations, an internal auditor may be employed by the organization.

The purposes of internal audits often vary significantly from the purpose of an external audit. As noted above, external audits are primarily focused on addressing the reliability of the organization's financial statements. Internal audits, however, may be designed to address either financial or operational matters. For example, an internal audit may be performed to assess an organization's compliance with its own operational policies in areas such as internal control, human resources, child safety, transportation safety, or other areas of significant interest [and potential risk] to the organization.

ATTRIBUTES OF A QUALITY INTERNAL AUDIT PROCESS

Regardless of who leads and carries out an internal audit process for an organization, certain attributes should exist with respect to any internal audit activity in order for the activity to be useful and credible:

- An internal audit process should be overseen by a person or group [the oversight body] that is independent with respect to the issues being addressed.

- The person or group performing the internal audit procedures and issuing the related reports [the internal auditor] should also be independent with respect to the issues being addressed.

- The internal auditor should report directly to the oversight body and not to the organization's management. While the internal auditor will certainly interact with the organization's management and employees in performing audit procedures, the internal auditor must issue and present reports directly to the oversight body in order for an internal audit process to maintain credibility.

[Practical note – if an internal auditor is an employee of the organization, he or she is subject to the organization's applicable employment and other policies (e.g., payroll matters, employee benefits matters, etc.). With respect to such matters, an employee-internal auditor is subject to the authority of the organization's management, so long as management's oversight does not interfere with or impede the objectivity of the internal auditor's work and reporting responsibilities.]

- The oversight body should establish and formally approve specific objectives of the internal audit process, the methodologies to be used, and the timing and nature of the reports to be issued.

- The internal auditor should conduct the internal audit procedures and prepare the related reports pursuant to the objectives and methodologies approved by the oversight body described in the preceding sentence.

- The internal auditor's reports should provide an <u>objective</u> description of the internal auditor's findings. The quality and credibility of an internal auditor's reports can be severely compromised when the internal auditor's report goes beyond reporting objective findings to drawing personal conclusions or making subjective statements of opinion regarding the matters subject to the audit.

[For example, if an internal auditor were to note in his report that the auditor observed certain children's classrooms being supervised by only one adult in violation of the organization's two-adult protocol, reporting such a finding in and of itself would be objective. If the internal auditor were to add a subjective statement such as, "These violations jeopardized the safety of our organization's children," or "The teachers responsible for these violations should be disciplined," the credibility and objectivity of the internal auditor's report would be compromised. Further, such statements could increase the organization's legal risks.]

ACCREDITATION

Another aspect of financial accountability that warrants consideration by the board is accreditation. For some nonprofit organizations (e.g., schools), accreditation by an independent accrediting body in the organization's field of service is a central expectation. In addition to accrediting bodies that operate in specific fields (education, health care, museums, etc.), there are independent accrediting bodies that accredit nonprofit organizations more generally in the areas of financial integrity, governance, and other key areas of operation. The Better Business Bureau's Wise Giving Alliance (www.give.org) is one such body that accredits eligible nonprofit organizations based on a system of 20 standards that address governance and oversight, effectiveness, finances, and fundraising. ECFA (www.ecfa.org) is an accrediting body that accredits certain Christian churches and ministries pursuant to a system of "Seven Standards of Responsible Stewardship." Uniquely, organizations are required to meet all of the ECFA Standards on an ongoing basis as a condition of continued accreditation. The ECFA Standards address doctrinal issues, governance, financial oversight, use of resources, compliance with laws, transparency, executive compensation, related party transactions, and fundraising practices.

A common element of the requirements for accreditation by an accrediting body is some form of engagement of a CPA firm to address the organization's financial activities. Commonly, that requirement is for an independent audit by the CPA firm of the organization's financial statements as described previously in this chapter.

One way or another, every responsible nonprofit organization should be able to demonstrate to its constituents appropriate accountability and a commitment to financial integrity. Accreditation by a credible, independent accrediting body can be an effective tool in demonstrating such a commitment.

4

KEY AREAS OF FINANCIAL OVERSIGHT

―――――――――― - - ――――――――――

Focusing on key areas will help the board address the issues most significant to the organization.

*Given the fact that an organization may decide, as described in **Chapter 2**, not to utilize a finance committee or its equivalent – and the reality that even if a finance committee is utilized, the governing body (board) of the organization is ultimately responsible for the affairs of the organization – this book generally refers to the board when referring to the financial oversight body. The fact that it does so is not intended to imply that a finance committee is not necessary or helpful for any particular organization. Rather, reference to the board is a practical means of simplifying the text for the reader.*

Responsibility for the financial oversight of a nonprofit organization can be a daunting duty for the board of an organization. In order to manage the breadth and scope of that responsibility, it is helpful to focus on and prioritize the key areas of an organization's financial activities requiring oversight. There is conceivably no limit to the amount of information that the board could attempt to evaluate and the amount of time it could take to do it. Focusing on key areas will help the board address the issues most significant to the organization, thereby making financial oversight a more manageable process.

PURPOSE OF THIS VERY BRIEF CHAPTER

The purpose of this very brief chapter is simply to identify the key areas of financial oversight for a board. Each of the keys areas is addressed in more detail in the following chapters.

GOVERNING DOCUMENTS AND POLICIES

The organization's governing documents – especially the bylaws – often contain provisions governing the financial oversight process. Additionally, the board of the organization determines what policies should be in place with respect to financial activities. These matters are addressed in **Chapter 5**.

INTERNAL FINANCIAL REPORTING AND MONITORING

In order for the board to effectively carry out its duty of financial oversight, it must have good and timely information. The board should determine the nature, format, and timing of the information it receives. This topic is addressed in **Chapter 6**.

FINANCIAL HEALTH

Clearly, the board must evaluate the financial health of the organization and ensure that it is both financially healthy and on track to remain so. The board must determine what metrics to use in evaluating financial health. **Chapter 7** addresses this topic.

TAX COMPLIANCE

Compliance with applicable tax law is critical for nonprofit organizations, since they rely significantly on various tax exemptions. Those tax exemptions must be protected. Additionally, even though nonprofits are often exempt from certain taxes, they are subject to others. An overview of the board's role with respect to tax compliance matters is provided in **Chapter 8**.

RISK MANAGEMENT

All organizational risk carries a financial component. For example, the risk that an organization's building could be damaged by fire is both a physical risk and a financial risk. Noncompliance with applicable laws can also have financial implications. Having an appropriate approach to overall risk management will help the board mitigate financial risks. This topic is the subject of **Chapter 9**.

5

GOVERNING DOCUMENTS AND POLICIES

Much "hooey" is communicated in this area of board governance.

Given the fact that an organization may decide, as described in **Chapter 2**, not to utilize a finance committee or its equivalent – and the reality that even if a finance committee is utilized, the governing body (board) of the organization is ultimately responsible for the affairs of the organization – this book generally refers to the board when referring to the financial oversight body. The fact that it does so is not intended to imply that a finance committee is not necessary or helpful for any particular organization. Rather, reference to the board is a practical means of simplifying the text for the reader.

Well-governed organizations will operate pursuant to a hierarchy of governing and policy documents. Such documents establish the parameters within which the organization, its board, and its staff leaders are to operate and are indispensable in establishing stability.

The legal hierarchy of governing and policy documents is not a matter of opinion or debate, but rather a matter of law. If a conflict exists among two or more documents in the hierarchy, the higher-level document trumps the others.

The hierarchy of documents is as follows:

- Law (federal, state, and local)
- Articles of incorporation
- Bylaws
- Policies (adopted by the board)
- Procedures (adopted by management)

LAW

The laws of the state in which the organization was incorporated establish the ultimate legal framework within which the organization must operate. Every state has such laws. Portions of state nonprofit corporation law apply regardless of the provisions in the organization's articles of incorporation or bylaws. For example, Florida Statutes Section 617.0833 prohibits loans by a Florida nonprofit corporation to its officers, directors, and certain other related parties, regardless of whether the organization's articles of incorporation or bylaws permit such loans.

Other portions of state nonprofit corporation law provide authority regarding certain matters, but defer to the organization's articles of incorporation or bylaws if they contain conflicting provisions. For example, Section 108.15(b) of the Illinois General Not For Profit Corporation Act states, "The act of the majority of the directors present at a meeting at which a quorum is present shall be the act of the board of directors, unless the act of a greater number is required by the articles of incorporation or the bylaws."

Since each state has unique laws covering employment, charitable solicitation, and other matters, nonprofit corporations incorporated in one state but operating in one or more other states should consult their legal counsel to determine which state laws apply or control. Additionally, local laws (often called "ordinances") should also be considered in the jurisdictions in which the organization operates.

Nonprofit organizations obtain their federal tax-exempt status through federal tax law, which dictates various criteria for obtaining and maintaining tax-exempt status. Tax-exempt organizations must take care to ensure compliance with applicable federal tax law in order to avoid losing their exemption. A detailed analysis of tax law compliance requirements is outside the scope of this book. However, as described in **Chapter 8**, the board should ensure that the organization proactively assesses the organization's compliance with applicable tax laws. Of course, compliance with other aspects of the law is important as well.

ARTICLES OF INCORPORATION

The articles of incorporation (sometimes referred to as the "charter") of a nonprofit corporation is the document that gives legal life to the organization. A corporation is a legal entity created by filing articles of incorporation with the appropriate state agency. The articles of incorporation are the highest-ranking governing document of the organization. Because the original document is filed with the state, amendments to the articles of incorporation must also be filed with the state. An organization's articles of incorporation and related amendments are public documents.

The articles of incorporation must contain certain minimum provisions under state law – typically the name and initial address of the organization, purpose language, an indication as to whether the organization has members, the names of initial board members, and the like. Additionally, a nonprofit organization that is or plans to be exempt from federal income tax as a charitable, religious, or educational organization described in Section 501(c)(3) of the Internal Revenue Code must include in its articles of incorporation certain provisions limiting the activities of the organization to those permitted for such exempt organizations.

It is permissible for an organization to include in the articles any amount of detail it wishes regarding the organization's governance. However, since all amendments to the articles must be filed with the state agency, it is common practice to make the articles of incorporation rather minimal in content and to include the organization's more detailed governance provisions in the bylaws, which are easier to amend and are not required to be filed with the state. Accordingly, the articles of incorporation rarely include specific provisions related to financial operations.

A nonprofit organization should consult legal counsel with significant nonprofit experience when drafting its original articles of incorporation or any amendments to them.

BYLAWS

The bylaws of an organization typically contain the specific governance provisions of the organization. Typical provisions in an organization's bylaws include, but are not limited to:

- Qualifications of members and process for joining (for organizations that have members);

- Qualifications for board members and terms of office;

- Process for the election and removal of board members and for filling board vacancies;

- Corporate officer titles, duties, responsibilities, election, removal, and terms of office;

- Information about the conduct of meetings, including quorum requirements and voting requirements (which may include supermajority voting requirements for certain matters);

- Indemnification of board members and officers with respect to liability stemming from the performance of their duties for the organization;

- The organization's fiscal year; and

- Requirements for amendment of the articles of incorporation and bylaws.

The organization should consult highly competent legal counsel for the drafting or amendment of its bylaws.

POLICIES

The nomenclature used in the area of "policies" varies dramatically in practice, so let's address that from the outset. The term "policies" can mean any number of things, including board resolutions, board-approved policy documents, management-approved documents, and more. Some distinguish between "board policies" and "management policies."

The author prefers to distinguish between the guiding documents approved by the board and those approved by management by referring to board-approved documents as "policies" and management-approved documents as "procedures." No clear right or wrong approach to nomenclature exists, but it is essential to distinguish between the two in some clear and appropriate manner.

For example, the board of a nonprofit adoption agency may establish a policy requiring that prospective employees who would serve in the financial operations area of the organization complete a criminal background check and have no record of felonies or crimes that would be a concern in connection with the proposed duties. The CEO may establish a procedure further clarifying the policy by requiring that the background check be national in scope and defining the specific types of criminal violations that are not acceptable for prospective financial employees. It is important that the distinction be made between the board's policy and the CEO's procedure so that, if the CEO wants to modify the list of unacceptable crimes, it is clear that he/she may do so without board approval, so long as the new procedure still complies with the board's policy.

The board is responsible for adopting and maintaining such policies as it believes are necessary and appropriate to establish parameters for the orderly operation of the organization. It is not necessary or advisable for the board's policies to replicate provisions that are included in the articles of incorporation or the bylaws, since doing so raises the risk that the documents will get out of sync at some point. The board should adopt only those policies that are truly necessary for the legal and orderly operation of the organization.

PROCEDURES

Management-adopted procedures represent guidance for the organization's staff under the leadership of the CEO. Procedures adopted by management should not conflict with board-approved policies or the organization's governing documents (articles of incorporation and bylaws). In fact, such procedures should typically address specific aspects of implementing the organization's board-approved policies or governing documents.

THE IMPORTANCE OF LEGAL COUNSEL

The board should ensure that highly competent legal counsel reviews all of the organization's governing and policy documents and advises the board regarding their propriety. Such a review should be conducted periodically to address changes that are made in the documents over time as well as changes that occur in the legal environment. Counsel should be involved in drafting and advising the board on *any* new policy considered by the board for adoption.

HOOEY ALERT!

Other than the requirements of state law and federal tax law for nonprofit organizations to include certain provisions in the articles of incorporation and bylaws as a condition for incorporation or tax exemption, there are rarely other legal requirements for nonprofit organizations to have specific board-approved policies. Much misinformation (hooey) is communicated in this area of board governance and much confusion exists as a result. The two primary sources of hooey in this area are:

- Those who state or imply that the *Sarbanes-Oxley Act*, which applies to publicly-traded companies, somehow applies in a similar fashion to nonprofit organizations; and

- The IRS.

SARBANES-OXLEY

Confusion often stems from the invalid assertion or implication in some nonprofit publications or other media that the *Sarbanes-Oxley Act* passed by Congress to govern the affairs of publicly-traded companies somehow applies to nonprofit organizations in the same manner that it applies to publicly-traded companies. <u>It does not</u>. Notwithstanding that fact, the nonprofit community is still rife with publications and presentations stating or implying otherwise. A simple Google search of the term "nonprofit" together with "Sarbanes-Oxley" will reap a mother lode of "resources" on the topic, along with litanies of recommendations regarding various policies that nonprofits "should" adopt.

It is true that two provisions of *Sarbanes-Oxley* apply to nonprofits – but the reason they do is because they apply to everyone in America! Those two provisions relate to:

1. Retaliating against a "whistleblower" – someone who reports illegal activity, and

2. Destroying, altering, or falsifying documents that are the subject of a federal proceeding.

Even with respect to these two provisions of the *Sarbanes-Oxley Act*, there is no requirement that nonprofits have certain policies in place. The Act simply makes it a federal crime to violate the whistleblower and record retention provisions of the law.

THE IRS AND POLICY REQUIREMENTS

The IRS is another source of rampant confusion regarding policy requirements for nonprofit organizations. After concluding that poor board governance was at the root of virtually all high-profile financial scandals that arose in the nonprofit sector in the past several decades, the IRS decided in the mid-2000s that nonprofit organizations should be pressured into adopting certain governance policies and practices.

In 2008, the IRS radically modified the annual federal information form that most nonprofits file (Form 990) to include numerous questions about whether the filing organization has adopted a variety of policies or practices related to its governance. The IRS added such questions to the form notwithstanding the fact that federal tax law contains no requirements for an organization to adopt such policies or practices as a condition of maintaining tax-exempt status.

As a result, a nonprofit organization filing Form 990 must now answer questions in this publicly-disseminated form such as:

- The number of the organization's board members who are "independent" (the IRS arbitrarily devised its own definition of independence for this purpose);

- Whether the organization has a conflicts-of-interest policy governing transactions between the organization and its insiders;

- Whether the organization has a whistleblower policy;

- Whether the organization has a record retention policy;

- Whether the organization's board reviews the Form 990;

- Whether the organization follows specific procedures in establishing executive compensation;

- Whether the organization has a policy covering executive expense reimbursements; and

- Whether the organization has a gift acceptance policy.

By adding such questions to the Form 990, the IRS knowingly created an environment of pressure for nonprofit organizations to adopt policies and practices that would allow them to answer "Yes!" Answering "yes" helps organizations avoid appearing to be recalcitrant. Many advisors in the nonprofit sector, the author included, believe that "no" answers to such questions raise the risk of an IRS audit.

In late 2009, the IRS announced that it would have its examination agents ask numerous questions about an organization's governance practices in every examination of nonprofit organizations for a period of time. Among the numerous issues the agents were to address was the attendance record of individual board members at board meetings! The IRS's apparent reason for obtaining such information during examinations is to document what it believes is the correlation between poor board governance and noncompliance with federal tax law.

As a result of the IRS's pressure, most large and respected nonprofit organizations have adopted policies and practices of the types addressed in the Form 990. Such policies, if drafted carefully in a manner that is appropriate for the organization, can be helpful, but they are not a requirement for tax exemption.

FAMILIARITY AND COMPLIANCE WITH GOVERNING AND POLICY DOCUMENTS

Every board member should read and be familiar with the organization's articles of incorporation, bylaws, and board-approved policies. Those documents provide the framework within which the board and management are to conduct their business. The board should ensure that the organization operates in compliance with its governing and policy documents. Failure to do so will likely result in a disorderly operating environment and can create significant legal problems for the organization and its leaders.

———————— - - ————————

WHAT FINANCIAL POLICIES SHOULD A NONPROFIT ORGANIZATION HAVE?

In determining whether a nonprofit organization's board should adopt a particular policy, the organization should consider several factors. Among them are:

- Whether the policy would be helpful in ensuring compliance with the law,

- Whether the policy could help protect the organization or its constituents,

- Whether the policy will enhance the effectiveness of the organization in carrying out its mission and purpose, and

- Whether the policy fosters confidence and trust on the part of supporters.

Philosophically, some organizations strive to minimize the number of formal policies they adopt. Once a policy is adopted, it requires monitoring and maintenance – to ensure that the policy is complied with and that the policy is kept up to date. Additionally, an argument can be made that the more policies an organization has, and the more specific those policies are, the greater the risk of failure to comply with those policies. From a risk management perspective, having a policy in place and failing to comply with it can sometimes create more exposure to liability than if the organization did not adopt the policy in the first place.

Many key areas of day-to-day financial operations can be governed by management-developed procedures without the need for board-adopted policies. For example, procedures for reimbursing business expenses, specific internal control practices, and procedures for managing accounts receivable collections can typically be adequately addressed by management-developed procedures.

The author suggests that financial policies for nonprofit organizations can be categorized into two groups:

- Policies that every nonprofit organization should probably have, and

- Policies that nonprofits should have if certain factors are present.

——————— - - ———————

Policies That Every Nonprofit Organization Should Probably Have

CONFLICTS-OF-INTEREST POLICY

A conflicts-of-interest policy addresses scenarios in which a person on the governing body (board) or otherwise in a position of leadership may benefit financially from a business arrangement or transaction involving the nonprofit organization. That can happen, for example, if the organization buys goods or services from the leader, from his company, from one or more of his family members, or from any of their companies. Other examples include selling items to one or more of these related parties, renting property to or from a related party, etc.

For good reason, federal tax law restricts the terms of certain transactions between tax-exempt nonprofit organizations and their leaders (or parties related to their leaders). Violations of federal tax law in this area can have dire consequences – not only for the organization but for the individuals involved in the transactions and the individuals who approve the transactions. Additionally, state nonprofit corporation laws also typically provide for adverse consequences if a nonprofit corporation engages in an improper transaction with a related party. Further, transactions between a nonprofit organization and its "insiders" can easily result in greater public scrutiny for the organization and adverse public relations.

Sometimes, a related party transaction may be economically advantageous to a nonprofit organization (for example, if a board member sells property to the organization for less than its value in order for the organization to build a necessary new facility). Even when a related party transaction is economically advantageous on its face, the organization should consider whether public perception of the transaction will be positive. And for some types of nonprofit organizations (e.g., private foundations), such a transaction is prohibited by federal tax law regardless of the fact that it is economically advantageous.

A well-drafted conflicts-of-interest policy prescribes how an organization and its leaders are to address potential business arrangements in order to ensure that they are proper and in the best interests of the organization.

See Appendix B for a sample conflicts-of-interest policy.

EXECUTIVE COMPENSATION-SETTING POLICY

Compensation arrangements for a nonprofit organization's top leaders have characteristics similar to the related party business transactions addressed above in the description of conflicts of interest. A leader should never be involved in the decision-making process with respect to his or her own compensation. As with related party business transactions, federal tax law sets forth parameters for permissible executive compensation by tax-exempt nonprofit organizations. As with other types of related party transactions, violations in the arena of executive compensation can have dire consequences.

A well-drafted executive compensation policy prescribes the process for setting executive compensation and documenting the process, along with the data supporting the decision.

See Appendix C for a sample executive compensation-setting policy.

DISHONESTY, FRAUD, AND WHISTLEBLOWER PROTECTION POLICY

While it might seem to go without saying, in today's culture it is a good idea to have a policy that specifically prohibits illegal activity, fraud, and other financial improprieties. Such a policy removes any doubt about whether such conduct in an organization is permissible. A dishonesty, fraud, and whistleblower protection policy both prohibits improper activity and prescribes the process by which an employee can report apparent improprieties. It also establishes the manner in which an organization addresses such reports. A provision of the Sarbanes-Oxley federal law prohibits retaliation by employers against workers ("whistleblowers") for reporting certain improprieties. A well-drafted policy will help an organization avoid violating this law.

> **See Appendix D for a sample dishonesty, fraud, and whistleblower protection policy.**

RECORD RETENTION POLICY

The federal *Sarbanes-Oxley* law includes provisions prohibiting the destruction or falsification of documents subject to certain federal proceedings. Additionally, federal tax law and other laws allow regulatory authorities to examine the records of nonprofit organizations for various reasons (compliance with employment law, employee benefits law, etc.). Such laws also require organizations to maintain appropriate records related to compliance with the laws. It is important for organizations to maintain records that may be required to be produced in the event of an IRS or other regulatory examination. Attorneys generally advise nonprofit organizations to adopt a record retention policy prescribing the types of records to be maintained and the duration of time that they will be maintained. In some cases, attorneys specifically advise that such policies require destruction of documents after the applicable retention period.

A record retention policy is necessarily unique to the type of organization adopting it. Additionally, different attorneys have very different views about the approach to record retention policies. (For example, some attorneys advocate strongly for purging records at the end of the required retention period and others do not.) For these reasons, we have not provided a sample record retention policy in this book. The author recommends that each organization's board adopt a record retention policy drafted uniquely for that organization under the specific advice of appropriately experienced legal counsel.

DONOR PRIVACY POLICY

In the current era of pervasive spam emails and data breaches, donors to nonprofit organizations are increasingly interested in knowing how their data will be used and protected once it is provided to the organization. It is considered a best practice in the nonprofit sector to have a donor privacy policy and to make that policy readily available to donors. Key elements of a donor privacy policy include informing the donor as to what kinds of information is gathered, how the information is used, whether it will be shared with others and under what terms, and how the donor may opt out of certain aspects of the organization's use of the data.

See Appendix E for a sample donor privacy policy.

POLICY REQUIRING BOARD APPROVAL FOR THE ISSUANCE OF DEBT AND OTHER FINANCIAL OBLIGATIONS

Many nonprofit organizations have provisions in the bylaws that require the board to approve issuance of any debt above a certain threshold or entering into any contractual obligation (e.g., a lease) to make ongoing payments in excess of a certain threshold. That is a good practice. An alternative to having such a provision in the bylaws is for the board to adopt a policy with such requirements. A bylaws provision or policy requirement could be worded along these lines:

Board approval is required for the issuance of any debt instrument with a principal amount in excess of $_____; for permitting any encumbrance, mortgage, or lien on any property or asset of the organization; or for entering into any contractual commitment not included in a board-approved budget to make ongoing payments (e.g., lease payments) totaling more than $_____. [If the board wishes to require a supermajority of the members of the board to approve such commitments, such a requirement should be included in the bylaws or policy. For example, the board may wish for such commitments to be approved by at least 75% of the board members currently holding office...as opposed to simply a majority of board members present at a meeting at which there is a quorum.]

POLICIES THAT NONPROFIT ORGANIZATIONS SHOULD HAVE IF CERTAIN FACTORS ARE PRESENT

GIFT ACCEPTANCE POLICY

A gift acceptance policy addresses an organization's practices for evaluating atypical gifts. Examples would be gifts accompanied by naming rights restrictions (e.g., that a particular building be named after the donor), gifts with restrictions not accommodated by existing restricted funds, gifts of real estate, gifts of personal property, gifts of ownership interests in privately held businesses, gifts of stock in foreign entities, etc. The policy should address what parties or groups in the organization have authority to evaluate and accept gifts covered by the policy and the factors or criteria to be considered in making such decisions.

A gift acceptance policy is appropriate for organizations that receive atypical gifts with some frequency. Even organizations that rarely receive such gifts may benefit from such a policy.

See Appendix F for a sample gift acceptance policy.

EXPENSE REIMBURSEMENT POLICY

As described previously in this chapter, the IRS Form 990 information return for nonprofit organizations includes a question about whether the organization has a policy for reimbursing its leaders for travel, meals, hospitality, and other expenses. While such a policy is not required by federal tax law, compliance with the law is, of course. Some organizations that are required to file Form 990 prefer to adopt such a policy, simply in order to be able to answer "yes" to the question. A well-drafted expense reimbursement policy will describe who is covered by the policy, parameters for expenses that will be paid or reimbursed by the organization, and documentation requirements. Whether an organization formally adopts such a policy or not, it should, of course, maintain practices that comply with applicable law.

See Appendix G for a sample expense reimbursement policy.

OTHER POLICIES

The policies described above are not intended to constitute an exhaustive list of financial policies that may be appropriate for an organization's board to adopt. Depending on the specific circumstances, additional policies may be helpful...or even necessary. Other policies that may be considered include, but are not limited to:

- **Any policies required as a matter of law for the particular type of organization.** The organization's legal counsel can help determine what specific policies may be required as a matter of law. (For example, federal tax law requires private, nonprofit, tax-exempt schools to adopt and apply a policy of racial nondiscrimination.)

- **Policy for spending restricted funds.** In order to avoid misunderstandings and possible conflicts, organizations that receive significant contributions restricted for particular purposes may benefit from a policy that clearly delineates who in the organization has the authority to spend the restricted funds.

- **Investment policy.** Organizations with significant investment portfolios should have an investment policy clearly describing the organization's investment risk tolerance and specific parameters for investment portfolio allocation. Nonprofit organizations should ensure that, among other things, their investment policy and practices are in conformity with applicable state law. Investment policies are, by their nature, specific to the organization, its risk tolerance, and its investment objectives. **(See Chapter 7 for more information about investment policies.)**

- **Joint venture policy.** For organizations that engage in joint venture activities with for-profit companies, a joint venture policy may be necessary to ensure compliance with applicable tax law. Organizations considering entering into joint venture arrangements should do so only under the advice of appropriately experienced legal counsel.

6

INTERNAL FINANCIAL REPORTING
AND MONITORING

———————— - - ————————

The solution is not to attempt to convert a board member or other leader into an accountant.

*Given the fact that an organization may decide, as described in **Chapter 2**, not to utilize a finance committee or its equivalent – and the reality that even if a finance committee is utilized, the governing body (board) of the organization is ultimately responsible for the affairs of the organization – this book generally refers to the board when referring to the financial oversight body. The fact that it does so is not intended to imply that a finance committee is not necessary or helpful for any particular organization. Rather, reference to the board is a practical means of simplifying the text for the reader.*

Why is it that in many nonprofit organizations, the members of the board, most or all of whom are not accountants, are given the organization's critical financial information in a format designed by accountants for accountants? The non-accountant board members are expected to be able to interpret financial statements, spreadsheets with rows and columns of numbers, and other similar reports – and use them to evaluate the organization's financial condition and activities. For some reason, many organizations have allowed themselves to have it *exactly backward* in terms of the way financial information is provided to board members. The board is not driving the nature and format of internal financial reporting...the accountants are!

An organization's internal financial reporting function is a *means*, not an end. Just as the driver of a car uses a variety of sources of information for the purpose of facilitating decision-making in driving toward the destination, a nonprofit organization's board uses financial reporting for the purpose of evaluating the organization's operations and activities. The accounting and financial reporting function serves a supporting and informational role with respect to the leadership and oversight of the organization.

Information provided by the financial reporting process must be <u>timely</u>, <u>accurate</u>, and <u>relevant</u>. A driver needs to know that his automobile is low on fuel before it is empty and he is stranded. Similarly, board members need timely, accurate, and relevant financial information in order to be apprised of current conditions. Financial information must meet <u>all three</u> of these attributes in order to truly be helpful to board members in carrying out their financial oversight duties.

Financial reports must also be <u>clear and understandable</u>. On occasion, a symbol may light up on a driver's dashboard that the driver doesn't recognize. While the symbol may indicate that something about the vehicle requires attention, if the driver doesn't know what the symbol means, it is of little value. Is tire pressure low? Is there a problem with the engine? Do I need to stop the car now? A mechanic at the repair shop may know what the symbol means, but that doesn't help the driver when he needs the information the most. And the driver can't carry the mechanic along with him on every trip. Similarly, financial reports must be provided to board members in a form and language that they understand. Financial reports that are presented in a highly detailed or technical format are often of limited value to board members. Accountants and others who prepare financial reports must take into consideration the fact that most board members (and in many cases, most finance committee members) are not accountants.

WHO SAYS INTERNAL FINANCIAL REPORTS MUST LOOK LIKE FINANCIAL STATEMENTS?

The terms "financial reports" and "financial statements" are not synonymous. Financial statements are a type of financial report but not every financial report is a financial statement. Internal financial reporting has as its primary purpose providing leaders with financial information that allows them to assess the financial condition of the organization, assess the financial results of its operating activities, and to make wise and informed decisions about the operations and activities of the organization. The nature, content, and format of internal financial reports provided to board members should facilitate their understanding and should *not* be in a format that only an accountant or financial professional can understand. Accordingly, it is likely that financial *statements* are among the <u>least</u> helpful financial reports to be used by board members. (It is true that if some members of the board or finance committee are trained financial professionals who know how to read and interpret financial statements, reporting financial information in the form of financial statements may be helpful to them. But what about the remainder of the board or finance committee? Is it not appropriate to provide them with financial information in a format that they understand?) Board and finance committee members need financial information presented in a user-friendly format, in plain language, and in a manner that highlights or otherwise directs attention to matters that require attention.

Additionally, the most helpful financial reporting information for board members is likely to include a combination of *financial and nonfinancial* information. Financial information alone presents an incomplete picture in many circumstances. For example, if a board member were to learn that contribution revenues increased for the first half of the year by 20 percent, that may sound like excellent news on its face. However, if the information about the 20 percent increase in contributions were accompanied by information indicating that one donor made a large gift accounting for more than the 20 percent increase, and that the number of donors giving had actually declined during the first half of the year, the organization's leadership would have a much more complete picture and would likely reach different conclusions.

With respect to internal financial reporting, there are no rules or laws that dictate the nature, scope, or format of the internal reports provided for the organization's leadership. Accordingly, financial reports should be presented in the manner which is most helpful to those who are using them. Graphs, charts, dashboard-like "gauges," and "plain-language" narratives are likely to provide the most helpful information in most circumstances.

ILLUSTRATION OF "GAUGES"

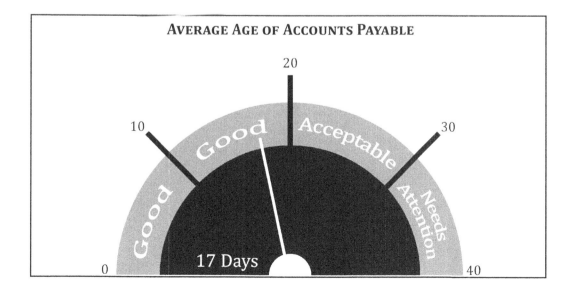

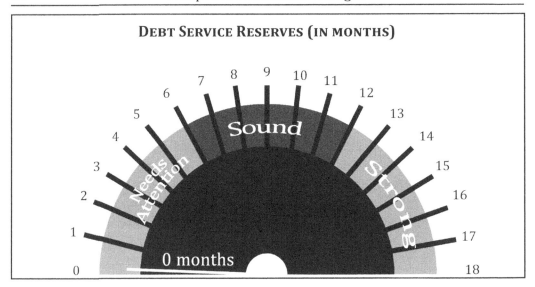

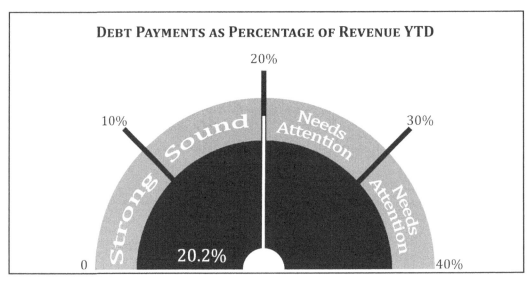

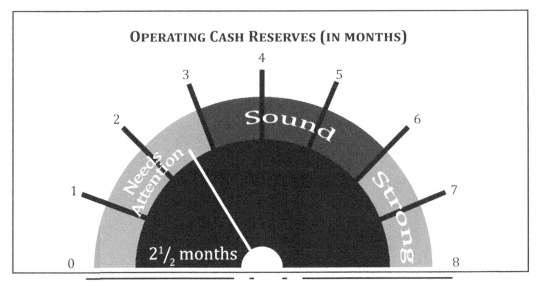

Illustration of "Plain-Language" Narrative Report

SAMPLE NARRATIVE REPORT ON LIQUIDITY AND FINANCIAL POSITION

The organization's overall financial position improved during the month of October as compared with September. Contribution revenue was $216,000 for the month of October as compared with approximately $184,000 for September. The operating cash balance has increased from approximately $430,000 at the end of September to approximately $470,000 at the end of October. The number of donors making a gift for October also increased to approximately 2,880 as compared to about 2,700 for September. The age of accounts payable invoices remains consistent at approximately 17 days. The organization continues to pay its bills in a timely manner. Debt payments as a percentage of overall revenue year-to-date is at approximately 20.2 percent, which is within the range the organization has deemed acceptable. Given the upward trending in giving, the overall outlook is good at this time.

We have not yet made meaningful progress toward achieving our goal of maintaining a debt service reserve equal to six months of debt service costs. We plan to begin to address that goal as part of the upcoming year's budgeting process.

What Information Should Be Covered by the Internal Financial Reporting Process?

KEY QUESTIONS

Board members and others charged with financial oversight should determine the nature and scope of information they need in order to carry out their respective responsibilities. An effective way to make such a determination is to identify "key questions" for which they will need answers as part of the ongoing financial reporting process. Once the key questions are identified, board members can evaluate and modify the financial reporting content and format to ensure that the financial reports adequately address the key questions. Following are examples of questions that nonprofit board members might incorporate into their list of key questions (the list is not intended to be exhaustive):

1. Is the organization's current liquidity sound or strong? On what do we base our opinion? How do we know?

2. Is the trending in the organization's liquidity improving or declining? Elaborate.

3. What is the organization's current balance for cash and other liquid assets overall? What is the balance net of donor-restricted and designated amounts? Provide details.

4. If current accounts payable and other similar liabilities were paid, how many months of cash operating expenses would the current cash and liquid assets balance (net of donor-restricted and designated amounts) cover?

   a. How does the answer to this question compare to the organization's objectives?

   b. Is there a plan in place to improve the operating cash reserves balance? What is the plan? How are we doing with respect to implementing the plan?

5. Is the organization paying all of its bills on time? How do we know?

6. Has the organization had any trouble in recent weeks or months meeting its cash flow demands? If yes, elaborate.

7. Does the organization expect to have any trouble in the foreseeable future with respect to meeting its cash flow demands? How do we know? If yes, elaborate.

8. Has the organization borrowed any money to fund regular operations or noncapital outlays? If yes, elaborate.

9. Has the organization dipped into donor-restricted or designated cash or investment balances in order to fund operations at any point during the last year? How do we know? If yes, elaborate.

10. What is the current balance of the organization's mortgage or long-term debt?

11. Are debt payments being made in a timely manner, without any difficulty?

12. Are there any specific financial covenants contained in the organization's loan agreements that stipulate specific financial requirements the organization must meet as a condition of complying with the terms of the loan? If yes, provide details with respect to the nature of each covenant as well as the organization's compliance with the terms of the covenant.

13. What percentage of the organization's total revenues is being spent on servicing the organization's debt?

   a. How does the answer to this question compare to the organization's objectives?

14. What is the ratio of the organization's total liabilities to the organization's unrestricted net assets?

   a. How does the answer to this question compare to the organization's objectives?

15. What is the balance of the organization's debt service reserves?

   a. How many months of debt service for the organization's existing mortgage debt will this balance cover?

   b. How does the answer to this question compare to the organization's objectives?

   c. Is there a plan in place to improve the debt service reserves balance? What is the plan? How are we doing with respect to implementing the plan?

16. Is there any information regarding the organization's overall liquidity or financial position not addressed by the above questions of which the organization's leadership should be aware? If yes, provide details.

17. Is the trending with respect to overall revenue favorable or declining?

   a. If declining, what are the causes, and what is the organization's leadership doing to address the matter?

18. Is per capita giving trending favorably or unfavorably? Provide details.

19. What other information about the organization's revenues (especially revenues not related to contributions) is relevant to organization leadership?

20. With respect to expenditures, is the organization's staff leadership adhering to budget parameters? How do we know?

21. Are expenditures increasing or decreasing?

22. Are appropriate approval processes in place for all expenditures? Elaborate and succinctly describe the approval process for all areas of expenditure.

23. Is there any additional information about the organization's expenditures not covered by the questions above that would be relevant to the organization's leaders?

24. Is the organization generating a cash flow surplus from its operating activities? Why or why not?

25. How do the organization's financial operating results compare with expectations as set forth in the approved budget?

26. Are there any current vulnerabilities, specific risks, threats, or other similar matters that could adversely affect the organization's financial condition? If yes, elaborate.

27. On a scale of 1 to 10, where 1 is very weak and 10 is extraordinarily strong, how would the organization's staff leadership rate the organization's current financial condition? Explain the basis for the rating.

***Note** – Responses to key questions should be provided in plain-language. A perfectly acceptable format for a portion of the organization's internal financial reporting may very well be a Q&A format where questions like those in the examples above are provided along with appropriate responses by members of the accounting and financial management team. Such a format can cover a particular period of time. Once responses are formulated to the questions, the responses can be updated each time new reports are required. If changes to the responses are <u>highlighted</u>, users of the reports can quickly and easily identify new information. Of course, the organization's accounting and finance team should have appropriate financial statements, schedules, and other details available to support the responses.*

BOARD MEMBERS SHOULD NOT SUCCUMB TO INTIMIDATION OVER FINANCIAL REPORTING

If a board member does not completely understand the internal financial reports that are being provided to him or her, or if he/she feels that he/she needs additional information beyond what he/she is receiving, that board member should work with the organization's board chair, treasurer, and

> *A board member should never be intimidated if he/she does not understand information in the financial reports.*

CEO to revise and improve the financial reporting process. A board member should never be intimidated if he/she does not understand information in the financial reports. If the board member does not adequately comprehend the financial reporting information he/she is receiving, that board member cannot carry out his or her responsibilities adequately and must address the issue appropriately.

THE BOTTOM LINE

The bottom line is this – effective internal financial reporting is always based on the premise that meaningful, usable, relevant, and timely information is provided to board members and others charged with financial oversight in a format that they can easily understand. When that is not happening, the solution is not to attempt to convert a board member or other leader into an accountant. Rather, the organization must adapt its financial reporting to the needs, language, and experience of those charged with financial oversight.

7

FINANCIAL HEALTH

———————— - - ————————

The financial health of a nonprofit organization is best measured with reference to its statement of financial position (balance sheet), with a focus on its assets and liabilities.

*Given the fact that an organization may decide, as described in **Chapter 2**, not to utilize a finance committee or its equivalent – and the reality that even if a finance committee is utilized, the governing body (board) of the organization is ultimately responsible for the affairs of the organization – this book generally refers to the board when referring to the financial oversight body. The fact that it does so is not intended to imply that a finance committee is not necessary or helpful for any particular organization. Rather, reference to the board is a practical means of simplifying the text for the reader.*

THE BOARD'S ROLE IN OVERSEEING FINANCIAL HEALTH

One of the most important aspects of the board's financial oversight responsibility is its obligation to continually monitor and evaluate the financial health of the organization. An organization must be financially viable in order to sustainably carry out its mission. In order for the board to effectively carry out its responsibility in this area, it must have perspective with respect to what constitutes a desirable financial condition. This is an area in which the board should have an active role. Determining what *should be* the financial condition of the organization is an appropriate role for the board as part of its responsibility to lead in the area of strategy for the organization. In other words, the board has a duty to determine the organization's desired financial condition as a key element of its role in financial oversight. It is impossible to determine whether an organization's financial condition is acceptable without having first defined what constitutes acceptable financial condition.

FINANCIAL HEALTH - A MATTER OF DEGREE AND PHILOSOPHY

Financial health for a nonprofit organization is a matter of degree and, to some extent, a matter of opinion. It is also a matter of philosophy. Some nonprofit organizations intentionally operate with razor-thin margins and no cash reserves. Sometimes, it is a matter of honor or even religious principle. Other organizations believe in operating with healthy financial margins and in maintaining reasonable cash reserves for unexpected developments. The author espouses the latter philosophy and the remainder of this chapter is written from that perspective.

ASSETS AND LIABILITIES

The financial health of a nonprofit organization is best measured with reference to its statement of financial position (balance sheet), with a focus on its assets and liabilities. Assets are items that the organization owns or has a claim to and that have some value. Liabilities are obligations of the organization. Some liabilities are "hard," meaning that the organization actually owes money or property to another party, and some liabilities are "soft," meaning that they represent some other form of obligation – often an obligation to perform a service for which the organization has already been compensated. Obviously, from an overall financial health perspective, the more assets an organization has the better, and the less liabilities an organization has the better. And not all assets or liabilities are equal. Assets in the form of cash or that can be readily converted into cash provide more liquidity and flexibility to the organization than do other types of assets. Liabilities that represent hard obligations to pay money in the near future impact an organization's liquidity and flexibility more than other types of liabilities.

TARGETS AND MEANS

In order for the board to effectively evaluate the financial condition of an organization, it must have targets – particularly targets that relate to the statement of financial position (balance sheet). We address some recommended targets later in this chapter. To the extent that an organization's financial condition is not where its board would like it to be, the board, together with the CEO, should develop and approve a plan for getting from Point A to Point B. Typically, that plan comes in the form of the organization's operating budget – which is to be developed by management and approved by the board. An organization that needs to improve its financial condition can only do so by bringing in more assets than it expends. (In other words, a nonprofit organization must generate a cash surplus from its operations in order to improve its financial condition and go from Point A to Point B.) A board interested in seeing that an organization's financial condition improves must engage in the budgeting oversight process to ensure that the budget plan includes a strategy for such improvement. The budget plan is the means for achieving an organization's financial condition targets.

The author notes here that a detailed description of the budgeting process is outside the scope of this book, as the process of developing a budget for the board's consideration is a role for the organization's management. The author recommends the book *Church Finance*, co-written by the author and attorney Richard Hammar and published by Christianity Today, which addresses in more detail the budgeting process, the multiple types of budgets that an organization may have, and numerous other related topics. Notwithstanding its title, the book *Church Finance* contains information helpful to nonreligious nonprofit organizations as well as churches and other religious organizations.

TIMETABLE – IT DOESN'T HAVE TO HAPPEN OVERNIGHT

Once the financial position targets are defined, the organization should establish what it considers to be a reasonable timeframe for achieving the objectives. For an organization that is a long way from achieving its objectives, it is wise not to attempt to get from Point A to Point B overnight. Depending on the circumstances, the process of reaching the organization's targets may take a number of years. If the organization believes its journey from Point A to Point B will be long-term, it is important for the board to establish annual benchmarks or milestones (interim targets) to facilitate the monitoring and assessment of progress.

For example, assume the organization has one month's cash operating expenses as a cash reserve and it plans to achieve a six-month reserve. Assume the board decides to achieve its target over a five-year period, by increasing the reserve by one month's operating expenses each year. The board establishes milestones for the end of each year accordingly. At the end of Year 1, the organization should have two months of operating expenses in its cash reserves. At the end of Year 2, it should have three months, and so on, until the end of Year 5, at which it should have six months of operating expenses in reserves, assuming the organization has been able to follow its plan.

Recommended Liquidity and Financial Position Targets

WHAT CONSTITUTES "REASONABLE" CASH RESERVES AND "SOUND" FINANCIAL POSITION FOR A NONPROFIT ORGANIZATION?

Based on more than 30 years of professional experience in the field and on communications with colleagues and other nonprofit financial professionals, the author provides the following observations and recommendations. The recommendations provided herein are general in nature and may not be appropriate for some organizations, depending on the individual facts and circumstances. The author also acknowledges that some may have differing opinions regarding the targets described below. The author respects such differences of opinion, noting, however, that in publicly espousing these targets over several years, the author has had no nonprofit leaders argue that the targets are inappropriate.

Sound refers to a level that represents the minimum position for establishing healthy liquidity and financial position. *Strong* refers to a level where financial position and liquidity should be more than adequate in most circumstances. The term "*cash*" as it relates to reserves and balances is intended to include liquid marketable investment securities.

OPERATING CASH RESERVES

(Note – The recommended levels are based on the assumption that the organization already maintains cash, including liquid marketable securities, adequate to cover all donor-restricted and designated net assets. Recommended reserves and balances are levels in excess of the amounts required to cover such items.)

Sound: Three months of operating cash expenses plus current liabilities

Strong: At least six months of operating cash expenses plus current liabilities

DEBT SERVICE RESERVES (FOR ORGANIZATIONS WITH MORTGAGE OR OTHER LONG-TERM DEBT)

Sound: Six months of debt service costs (principal and interest payments)

Strong: At least one year of debt service costs

(Note – If a lender requires maintenance of minimum debt service reserves, the actual use of the lender-required reserves will typically create an event of default on the loan if the use of the funds causes the reserve balance to decrease below the required minimum. Accordingly, the organization should maintain debt service reserves above and beyond the level required by a lender if the organization wishes to be able to access the reserves without defaulting on the loan.)

DEBT LEVEL

Sound: Total liabilities do not exceed 2.5 times the organization's unrestricted net assets.

Strong: Total liabilities are less than 2 times the organization's unrestricted net assets.

LOAN TO VALUE RATIO

Sound: Debt does not exceed 70% of the current market value of the underlying property that collateralizes it.

Strong: Debt is less than 65% of the current market value of the collateral property.

DEBT SERVICE

Sound: Annual debt service payments (principal and interest) do not exceed 15-20% of the organization's annual cash operating expenses.*

Strong: Annual debt service payments do not exceed 10% of the organization's annual cash operating expenses.*

*To the extent that debt service payments are made from operating expenses. Debt service payments funded by special gifts or separate funds, such as a building fund or debt service fund, would not be counted in this calculation.

AVERAGE AGE OF ACCOUNTS PAYABLE INVOICES

Sound: Accounts payable invoices should not generally be more than 30 days old if the organization is paying its bills in a timely manner. Accordingly, the average age of accounts payable invoices should not exceed about 25 days.

If the average age of accounts payable invoices increases much beyond 25 days, the organization's leadership should consider that a warning sign of potential cash flow issues.

Strong: The average age of accounts payable invoices is not more than 15 days.

OTHER BENCHMARKS, RATIOS, INDUSTRY DATA, ETC.

The author considers the benchmark metrics described above to be among the most important for nonprofit organizations to monitor and pursue for sound liquidity and financial position. Organizations may find other measurements useful in their financial and other operations. In some cases, comparisons of an organization's data with industry data may be useful, such as when comparing the organization's salaries for key positions to information in salary surveys. In other cases, industry data may have limited usefulness, since nonprofit organizations are as unique as the individuals who comprise them. For example, it might be interesting to know how a particular organization stacks up against a peer group in the area of occupancy costs as a percentage of the operating budget or total personnel costs as a percentage of the operating budget. However, individual organizations making up a peer group will have widely varying facts and strategies in such areas. Some organizations own their facilities with no debt and will have minimal occupancy costs. Others may have new facilities built with borrowed money – along with heavy depreciation and interest expense. Yet other organizations may rent their facilities and have little or no maintenance costs. When it comes to personnel costs, some nonprofits espouse a heavily staff-centric model and believe in compensating their employees commensurately with the business world. Other organizations extensively utilize volunteers and believe that their employees should accept lower compensation as part of their service to the organization. With such wide disparities in facts, strategies, and philosophies among nonprofit organizations, it is extremely difficult if not impossible to use peer group data for validly assessing the reasonableness or appropriateness of an individual organization's financial operations.

Even if the peer group to which an organization compares itself is extraordinarily homogeneous, the fact that a group of nonprofit organizations spends 48% on average, for example, of their budgets on personnel costs means just that. It doesn't necessarily mean that such a spending level is appropriate for a particular organization. Such a determination would be based on the facts, philosophy, mission, and objectives of the particular organization. If an organization were to use the peer group average as a target, that would mean that the organization is targeting to be *average*. Is that really the right strategy for the organization?

Accordingly, an organization interested in tracking financial measurements and benchmarks may find the most useful information by comparing the organization's own numbers against the standard liquidity and financial condition metrics described above...and doing so over time. An organization may also benefit from comparing certain of its own key operating metrics (such as occupancy costs and personnel costs as a percentage of the budget) over time. For example, an organization may find it valuable to track the percentage of its operating expenses spent on personnel costs over a several-year period in order to determine whether the percentage is trending higher or lower.

Whatever methods or measurements are employed, nonprofit boards and staff leaders should assess the tools and benchmarks that will be most relevant and helpful given their organization's unique identity.

A WORD ABOUT CHARITY RATINGS ORGANIZATIONS

Some nonprofit organizations are subject to being "rated" by one or more self-appointed charity ratings organizations. The most well-known organization in that space is Charity Navigator, which rates certain nonprofit charities based on a model that takes into consideration a number of financial factors – some quantitative and some qualitative (e.g., availability of information, whether the organization has adopted certain policies, etc.). Charity Navigator's ratings are expressed in terms of a number of "stars" given to a charity, with the maximum being four stars. Regardless of one's opinion about the virtue of charity ratings and the organizations that issue them, they are a real force in the philanthropic marketplace and they do affect giving by some donors and grant funders. Nonprofit boards should determine whether their organization is or will be subject to rating by such an organization and, if so, how the ratings are determined. The board, together with management, should evaluate the organization's strategy with respect to its rating – and if the board wishes to optimize the organization's rating, it should ensure that appropriate steps are taken to do so.

OVERSIGHT OF INVESTMENTS

Nonprofit organizations that maintain cash reserves sometimes choose to invest in marketable securities in order to pursue increased returns on their investments, especially given the low interest rates that are often paid by banks on deposit accounts. Organizations that maintain investment portfolios must take care to invest prudently.

At the time this publication went to press, every state in the United States except Pennsylvania had adopted a version of the Uniform Prudent Management of Institutional Funds Act (UPMIFA), a model law developed by the Uniform Law Commission. UPMIFA establishes legal requirements for nonprofit organizations related to the investment and management of "institutional funds." The term "institutional funds" is defined very broadly and, for all practical purposes, includes virtually all cash and investments maintained by a nonprofit organization. The organization's board should ensure, under the advice of legal counsel, that the organization's investment practices comply with applicable state law.

INVESTMENT PHILOSOPHY

Before an organization decides on the specific investments to be included in its portfolio, the organization's board should first agree on a philosophy with respect to the organization's investing activities. An organization's investment philosophy should be expressed in general terms, should be in writing, and should be officially approved by the board.

In adopting an investment philosophy, the organization's primary considerations are its investment objectives and its risk tolerance. For example, the organization may express its desire for moderate growth and income potential together with low volatility and low risk of significant decreases in value. It is important for the investment philosophy to clearly articulate the board's investment objectives in order to guide the organization's investment *policy*.

INVESTMENT POLICY

Once the organization's leaders have adopted an appropriate statement reflecting its investment philosophy, the organization should adopt a more specific document that describes in more detail the nature of the investments to be held by the organization and the allocation of the organization's investment assets to particular categories of investments. Such a document is commonly referred to as an investment policy. Unless the organization has leaders with significant investment expertise participating directly in the process, the organization may wish to engage the services of an investment advisor or consultant in

> *Unless the organization has leaders with significant investment expertise participating directly in the process, the organization may wish to engage the services of an investment advisor or consultant in developing an appropriate investment policy.*

developing an appropriate investment policy. The investment policy should conform to the objectives and risk tolerance expressed by the organization in its investment philosophy statement described above. The investment policy will apply the principles from the investment philosophy statement to specific assets – commonly, in the form of asset allocation parameters. For example, an investment policy statement may dictate the percentage of the organization's investment portfolio to be invested in asset categories such as growth equities, value equities, government debt securities, corporate debt securities, real estate securities, commodities, international investments, etc. It is also common for investment policy statements to provide more specificity in each of these categories. For example, the policy may provide for specific levels of investment in short-term, intermediate-term, and long-term corporate debt securities. Once an investment policy is drafted, it should be approved by the organization's board.

In addition to addressing the matters described in the preceding paragraph, the organization's investment policy should also include provisions designed to remind those responsible for the organization's investments of the requirements of applicable law, such as UPMIFA (see above). Accordingly, some organizations include certain UPMIFA requirements in their investment policy document - a practice recommended by the author. Additionally, the organization's investment policy document should be reviewed and approved by the organization's legal counsel before it is adopted in its final form.

THE BOARD'S ROLE WITH RESPECT TO DEBT

Debt is like a chainsaw. It is a powerful tool that can help an organization do big things that it would otherwise not be able to do. It can also cut off your leg. Because debt is such a powerful tool, a nonprofit organization's

> *Debt is like a chainsaw.*

board *must* be engaged in the oversight of its use. The key roles of the board with respect to debt are to approve the issuance of any significant debt and to carefully monitor the handling of debt after its issuance.

Many nonprofit organizations have policies or provisions in the bylaws (see **Chapter 5**) that require the board to approve issuance of any debt above a certain threshold or entering into any contractual obligation (e.g., a lease) to make ongoing payments in excess of a certain threshold. That is a good practice. In deciding whether to approve issuance of debt, the board should take into consideration all relevant factors and trends, including its impact on the organization's liquidity and financial condition metrics (see above).

The board should understand and carefully evaluate the terms of the debt, including any specific *financial covenants* that may be included in the terms. Financial covenants are provisions requiring the borrower to meet certain financial conditions in addition to making the debt payments on time. Financial covenants are an important part of the terms of any debt, and they can easily be overlooked. The board should be comfortable that the organization will be able to comply with all of the terms of the debt before agreeing to issue it.

OVERALL COMMON SENSE PERSPECTIVE

No book or guide can address all aspects of financial health that a board should consider or monitor. Any organization would be well-served to have financial expertise on its board (or if it has one, its finance committee). There is no substitute for overall evaluation of an organization's financial health by people with significant financial expertise from a common sense perspective. Such perspective can help a board identify financial matters that need attention before they become problems.

8

Tax Compliance

_____ - - _____

A nonprofit's board should be keenly aware of certain tax compliance matters.

*Given the fact that an organization may decide, as described in **Chapter 2**, not to utilize a finance committee or its equivalent – and the reality that even if a finance committee is utilized, the governing body (board) of the organization is ultimately responsible for the affairs of the organization – this book generally refers to the board when referring to the financial oversight body. The fact that it does so is not intended to imply that a finance committee is not necessary or helpful for any particular organization. Rather, reference to the board is a practical means of simplifying the text for the reader.*

Nonprofit organizations enjoy various exemptions from federal, state, and local taxes. Charitable, religious, educational, scientific, or literary organizations described in Section 501(c)(3) of the Internal Revenue Code qualify for federal income tax exemption and enjoy a status that permits contributions to them to be deducted by donors for federal income tax purposes. Many federally tax-exempt organizations also have exemptions from state income taxes, state sales taxes, property taxes, and other taxes, depending on the facts and the laws in their jurisdictions. A nonprofit organization's tax exemptions are highly valuable and should be protected.

One might assume that a nonprofit, *tax-exempt* organization has little to be concerned with in the tax arena. In reality, it's not quite that simple. The compliance requirements to qualify for and maintain tax exemption must be heeded. In some cases, the exemptions require a renewal application process which must be monitored. Additionally, even though nonprofits may have exemptions from certain taxes, there are often other taxes which can and do apply. For example, virtually all nonprofit organizations that have employees are subject to the employer's Social Security and Medicare tax on employee wages. Additionally, a nonprofit organization that engages in certain types of business activities unrelated to its exempt purposes may be subject to federal and state income taxes. And there are other types of taxes that can apply as well. So, there is more than meets the eye when it comes to nonprofits and tax compliance.

THE BOARD'S APPROACH TO COMPLIANCE

The board should ensure that management applies appropriate safeguards to protect the organization's tax exemptions and otherwise comply with applicable tax law. One of the best ways an organization can ensure appropriate tax compliance is to engage the services of a CPA firm highly experienced in tax compliance matters for nonprofit, tax-exempt organizations. The organization should ensure that the members of the CPA firm specifically assigned to the organization are, themselves, highly experienced in such matters, and a clear understanding should exist between the firm and the organization that the CPA firm is specifically expected to *proactively* help the organization maintain its tax compliance. It is one thing for a CPA firm to serve an organization *reactively* by responding to tax compliance questions or issues raised by the organization. It is quite another for the CPA firm to proactively address tax compliance questions – many of which an organization may not know to ask. Well-governed nonprofit organizations should seek out and engage a firm that employs the latter service model.

KEY AREAS OF COMPLIANCE

As mentioned above, numerous tax compliance matters can apply to a nonprofit organization. An overview of the entire landscape of tax compliance for nonprofits is outside the scope of this book. However, a nonprofit's board should be keenly aware of certain tax compliance matters. A few tax compliance areas are among the most important and **relate directly to the board's oversight role** – specifically, the areas of:

- Executive compensation-setting,

- Related party transactions,

- Payroll tax withholding and remittance, and

- IRS Form 990.

These key areas of tax compliance are addressed with some specificity below.

Executive Compensation-Setting

The approach a nonprofit organization takes to executive compensation-setting is extremely important for a number of reasons. Two very significant reasons that executive compensation-setting practices are important are tax compliance and public relations. Under federal tax law, a leader of a nonprofit 501(c)(3) organization who is compensated excessively can be subjected to severe financial penalty taxes, as can organizational leaders who approve excessive compensation.

> *Two very significant reasons that executive compensation-setting practices are important are tax compliance and public relations.*

Scrutiny can come from a variety of sources – from the traditional news media, from bloggers, from tax authorities, or sometimes from an organization's own constituents. The ability to provide solid, well-developed responses to scrutiny can often determine whether the inquiring party will pursue the matter any further.

The manner in which a nonprofit organization handles compensation-setting for its leaders – especially its top leader – has a huge impact on the organization's preparedness for scrutiny in this sensitive area of operations. And the reality is that, barring highly unusual circumstances, the actual amount of the leader's compensation is far less important than the process and documentation employed by the organization in determining it.

The author has assisted nonprofit organizations in addressing inquiries from news reporters about executive compensation. In every case, where the organization was well-prepared and had robust systems in place, and where the organization responded positively and with confidence, the reporter's interest in the story quickly waned. It is important to communicate with confidence, making it clear that the organization has nothing to hide. Where there is no scandal, there is often no story.

For some organizations, risks related to executive compensation are low because executive compensation is well within the bounds of reasonableness in the eyes of any rational observer. For an organization where that is not true, however, the risk is greater, as is the need for a higher level of preparedness by the organization's board.

Additionally, for organizations like churches and church-affiliated organizations that do not file publicly available Form 990, information about the top leader's compensation may not be public. In such cases, the organization should still be prepared for inquiries about the leader's compensation. There may be no useful reason to disclose the amount of the compensation in such circumstances, but being able to describe a well-designed, robust, independent process for setting it could be very helpful.

WHEN THE REPORTER CALLS

It's hard to imagine which would be worse for a nonprofit organization – a half-baked news article improperly accusing the organization of paying its CEO too much, or one of the organization's board members being quoted in the article saying, "Wow, that's the first time I have heard he was being paid that much!" Sadly, such things do happen, and the purveyors of such articles are no longer limited to traditional news outlets. Social media, and especially "blogs," are an increasingly significant source.

Imagine, for example, the different outcomes likely to occur in each of the following scenarios. Assume that in both scenarios, the organization is a disease research organization and the CEO's total compensation is $300,000 per year. The organization files Form 990 annually. A reporter has reviewed the organization's most recent Form 990, having downloaded it from the GuideStar website (where 990s filed with the IRS are posted for public access).

SCENARIO 1

The newspaper reporter calls the organization and asks for the person who handles questions related to the CEO's compensation. The receptionist forwards the call to the CEO. The reporter tells the CEO that she has performed research on the CEO's pay as compared to other nonprofits in the area and has determined that the CEO is paid much more than his counterparts in the area. The CEO becomes defensive and says, "We don't have any comment other than to say that the compensation of all our people is reasonable – we follow all laws." The reporter obtains a list of the organization's board members and contacts one of them. The board member expresses surprise at the amount of the CEO's pay as cited by the reporter and says, "I don't really have anything to do with that. Our executive committee handles the CEO's pay, and the chair of that committee (and the board) is Sue Ross." The reporter then contacts Sue Ross, who says the organization determined that the CEO has had strong performance for the last few years and deserves the significant raises he has received. Sue notes that the CEO has led the organization in several areas of innovation. When asked about why the CEO is paid so much more than other nonprofits in the area, Sue responds again with commentary on the CEO's excellent performance.

SCENARIO 2

The newspaper reporter calls the organization and asks for the person who handles questions related to the CEO's compensation. The receptionist forwards the call to the CEO. The reporter tells the CEO that she has performed research on the CEO's pay as compared to other nonprofits in the area and has determined that the CEO is paid much more than his counterparts in the area. The CEO cheerfully says, "We have a very robust executive compensation-setting process, and it is headed up by Sue Ross, the chair of our board's compensation committee. Let me send you a copy of our executive compensation policy and I will ask Sue to give you a call." The reporter receives the policy, which states that the board has established an independent compensation committee made up entirely of board members with no conflicts of interest regarding the CEO's compensation. The policy requires the committee to commission a study at least every three years, comparing the CEO's compensation package with that of comparable organizations. The study is to be performed by an outside independent compensation expert. The committee is required to review the study and then recommend to the full board the CEO's compensation package in light of the study's results. The full board must approve the CEO's compensation package on an annual basis. Sue calls the reporter and advises her that the organization has carefully followed the policy and the most recent compensation study was completed a year ago. Sue explains that, due to the nature of the organization's work in disease research, the organization requires that the CEO have a doctorate in a particular field of pathology. The CEO, a PhD, was hired from a teaching hospital and is actually compensated at a level that is lower than that suggested by the independent study performed for the organization. Sue finishes her commentary by noting that the CEO's compensation may differ from that of other organizations in the area, but the organization, its CEO, and the CEO's credentials are unique in the area. Sue provides the names of similar organizations elsewhere in the country, all of which compensate their CEO at levels comparable to or above that of the local CEO – a fact that can be verified by a review of their Forms 990.

While the CEO's compensation level may be the same in both scenarios described above, the outcomes would likely be very different. Preparedness for scrutiny should be a key element of a nonprofit board's diligence in the area of executive compensation-setting – especially if the top leader is highly compensated.

BEST PRACTICES IN SETTING EXECUTIVE COMPENSATION

Best practices in setting compensation for an organization's top executive (referred to herein as "the CEO") include the following:

1. The compensation should be evaluated and established by the organization's board of directors (or equivalent) or a committee authorized by the board. The board or committee should be composed entirely of people who have no conflict of interest with respect to determining the CEO's compensation (e.g., no family members of the CEO, no subordinates of the CEO, no individuals whose compensation is determined by the CEO, etc.). [If such persons serve on the board and the board is the compensation-setting body, they should be excused from the CEO compensation-setting process.]

2. The board or committee should obtain valid comparability data reflecting what similar organizations pay similarly qualified people for performing similar duties. Comparability data may come from surveys (if readily available for comparable organizations), from Forms 990 of comparable organizations, or from other sources such as privately commissioned executive compensation studies.

3. The board or committee should contemporaneously document its decision about the CEO's compensation, including (if applicable) justification for approving compensation above that suggested by the comparability data.

4. The full board of directors (or equivalent) should generally be made aware of or should approve the CEO's total compensation package on an annual basis. [Churches and church-related organizations may follow church polity regarding the group or body charged with knowing and approving executive compensation.] If a committee is utilized, the board should determine the extent to which the full board should be involved in the process.

5. The organization should have a well-developed and clear communications plan for responding to inquiries about the compensation of its leadership.

Preparedness and diligence in executive compensation-setting are well worth the effort – a fact that becomes readily apparent when a reporter calls or the IRS announces that it plans to examine your organization.

See Appendix C for a sample executive compensation-setting policy.

Related Party Transactions

The federal tax laws that limit nonprofit leader compensation to a reasonable level also apply to transactions between 501(c)(3) [and certain other] nonprofit organizations and their related parties. As described in **Chapter 5**, a conflicts-of-interest policy addresses scenarios in which a person on the governing body (board) or otherwise in a position of leadership may benefit financially from a business arrangement or transaction involving the nonprofit organization. That can happen, for example, if the organization buys goods or services from the leader, from his/her company, from one or more of his/her family members, or from any of their companies. Other examples include selling items to one or more of these related parties, renting property to or from a related party, etc.

For good reason, federal tax law restricts the terms of certain transactions between tax-exempt nonprofit organizations and their leaders (or parties related to their leaders). Violations of federal tax law in this area can have dire consequences – not only for the organization but for the individuals involved in the transactions and the individuals who approve the transactions. Additionally, state nonprofit corporation laws also typically provide for adverse consequences if a nonprofit corporation engages in an improper transaction with a related party. Further, transactions between a nonprofit organization and its "insiders" can easily result in greater public scrutiny for the organization and adverse public relations.

Sometimes, a related party transaction may be economically advantageous to a nonprofit organization (for example, if a board member sells property to the organization for less than its value in order for the organization to build a necessary new facility). Even when a related party transaction is economically advantageous on its face, the organization should consider whether public perception of the transaction will be positive. And for some types of nonprofit organizations (e.g., private foundations), such a transaction is prohibited by federal tax law regardless of the fact that it is economically advantageous to the organization.

A well-drafted conflicts-of-interest policy prescribes how an organization and its leaders are to address potential business arrangements in order to ensure that they are proper and in the best interests of the organization.

See Appendix B for a sample conflicts-of-interest policy.

Payroll Tax Withholding and Remittance

Payroll tax withholding and remittance is a relatively simple but critically important compliance area for board oversight. In short, taxes withheld from an employee's pay must be submitted to the appropriate tax authorities very promptly – within very short timelines prescribed by law (typically, a few days). Federal and state laws treat the matter of making payroll tax deposits timely very seriously – as they should – since the funds withheld are the funds of the employee and the employer is entrusted with depositing them promptly and correctly.

Failure to deposit payroll taxes on time can result in very significant financial penalties. Failure to deposit them for an extended period can cause the organization's liability to increase dramatically. Under federal tax law, a

> *Willful failure to make proper payroll tax deposits is a felony, with a possible prison sentence.*

100% penalty can also be applied to "responsible persons," which, in some cases, can include officers or board members. Additionally, willful failure to make proper payroll tax deposits is a felony, with a possible prison sentence. The IRS enforces payroll tax compliance aggressively.

The board should implement an appropriate monitoring mechanism which allows it to determine compliance with applicable payroll tax deposit requirements. That mechanism could be as simple as a periodic written representation from management affirming that all required payroll tax deposits have been timely made...or, if the board wishes to employ a more rigorous procedure, a member or committee of the board can periodically inspect the payroll tax deposit records and report the results to the board.

IRS Form 990

For a nonprofit organization required to file it, no document the organization produces is likely to have more potential to affect the organization, its donors, and its other stakeholders than IRS Form 990.

Form 990 is an annual information return that must generally be filed with the Internal Revenue Service by most tax-exempt organizations, including 501(c)(3) public charities (other than churches and certain church-related organizations). Small nonprofits (those with annual revenues normally less than $200,000 and assets less than $500,000) are permitted to file a somewhat abbreviated version of Form 990 (Form 990-EZ), and very small organizations (those with annual revenues normally not more than $50,000) must file a simple notice with the IRS electronically each year.

THE PURPOSE AND USE OF FORM 990

The primary purpose of Form 990 is to report information about an organization's activities to the Internal Revenue Service. The IRS uses the information to assess the organization's compliance with applicable laws and to identify issues that may require further attention. Information provided by an organization on Form 990 may be the basis for an IRS inquiry or examination.

Form 990 is required to be made available for public inspection by the filing organization and by the IRS. The IRS provides copies of all Forms 990 that it receives to the nonprofit organization GuideStar, which in turn, makes the forms public on the **www.GuideStar.org** website shortly after they are filed with the IRS.

In addition to being used by the IRS as described above, information in Form 990 is used by a variety of other parties in multiple ways:

- The public and the media use Form 990 to access information about an organization's activities to form a perception of the organization. The perception developed can affect media coverage of the organization and giving decisions by the public. Typically, the media and members of the public have the highest level of interest in the Form 990 disclosures about compensation of the organization's leaders and business transactions with related parties.

- Charity "watchdog" groups use information in Form 990 to evaluate and rate nonprofit organizations. The most well-known example is Charity Navigator, an organization that rates 501(c)(3) charities using a "star" system based heavily on an organization's financial information and practices as described in Form 990. Grant-funding organizations and donors are sometimes influenced by the ratings of charitable organizations by such watchdog groups. Charity watchdog groups tend to focus heavily on organizations' overhead expenses, fundraising expenses, executive compensation and benefits, and related party transactions.

- Nonprofit organizations that solicit contributions are often required to submit a copy of their annual Form 990 to state government officials in connection with state charitable solicitation registration. As a result, the Form 990 often becomes accessible to the public within the applicable state agency's records in addition to being publicly available through the IRS or on the GuideStar website.

THE DEPTH AND BREADTH OF FORM 990

In addition to requiring exhaustive financial information, Form 990 requires organizations to disclose significant information about their governance procedures and policies, governing documents, relationships with their organizational leaders and with third parties, and much more.

Part I of Form 990 includes inquiries into the following:

- Number of independent voting members of the governing body

- Number of non-independent voting members of the governing body

- Number of employees

- Number of volunteers

- Total unrelated business income

- Revenue in the form of contributions and grants

- Program service revenue

- Investment income

- Expenses in the form of grants

- Benefits to or for members

- Salaries

- Fundraising fees

Part III of Form 990 asks the filing organization to describe its:

- Mission

- Largest (in terms of expenses) three "Program Service Accomplishments"

- Total expenses

Part VI of Form 990, entitled "Governance, Management, and Disclosure," is a detailed inquiry into the organization's governance and management.

Part VII of Form 990 requires reporting on:

- Compensation of officers

- Compensation of directors

- Compensation of trustees

- Compensation of key employees

- Highest compensated employees

- Compensation of independent contractors

A number of additional schedules may also apply, depending on the filing organization's activities, including schedules detailing information about:

- The identity of the organization's largest donors;

- Lobbying activities;

- Activities conducted outside the United States;

- Grants and other assistance made;

- Compensation for certain officers, directors, individual trustees, key employees, and highest compensated employees;

- Certain compensation practices;

- Financial transactions or arrangements between the organization and related parties; and

- Much more.

To say that Form 990 requires detailed reporting about an organization's activities is a significant understatement. Even the summary provided above does not begin to adequately describe the depth and breadth of the information required to be disclosed on Form 990.

Form 990 Also Presents an Opportunity to Share Positive Information

The highly public nature of Form 990 provides filing organizations with free publicity – and therewith an opportunity to present positive information about the organization and its activities. Some of the questions in Form 990 present unique opportunities to share information about the organization's mission and purpose, the positive impact of its activities, and the effectiveness of its programs. Nonprofit organizations should use these opportunities well.

The Sobering Implications of Filing an Incorrect or Incomplete Form 990

Form 990 is signed by an organization's officer "under penalties of perjury." Federal law allows the IRS to assess significant penalties on an organization and/or its leaders for providing incorrect or incomplete information in Form 990. Additionally, it is a federal criminal offense to knowingly submit false information on Form 990 to the Internal Revenue Service. Given the expansive amount of information and the exhaustive number of questions on Form 990 and its related schedules, the potential for providing incorrect information is significant.

When Form 990 is provided by an organization to state agencies in connection with charitable solicitation registration, state-level requirements for truthfulness typically apply. Most states have laws that prohibit an organization from providing false or misleading information in connection with fundraising solicitations made within the state. State government officials may apply such statutes to an organization soliciting funds in the state if the state learns that information in Form 990 submitted to the state is incorrect or incomplete.

REVIEW OF FORM 990 BY THE BOARD

Best practices dictate that a copy of Form 990 should be provided to the organization's board for review prior to filing with the IRS. In fact, a question on the Form 990 asks whether the organization provides a copy of the completed form to all members of its governing body before filing it. The form also requires the organization to describe the process used by the organization to review the Form 990. There are good reasons for an organization's board members to review the Form 990, including the fact that doing so helps the board maintain an awareness of important details and aspects of the organization's operations. If any board member reviewing the form has questions or concerns about its content, he/she should address those matters with the board chair and the CEO promptly.

9

RISK MANAGEMENT

---- - - ----

An effective risk management plan is a holistic one.

Given the fact that an organization may decide, as described in **Chapter 2**, *not to utilize a finance committee or its equivalent – and the reality that even if a finance committee is utilized, the governing body (board) of the organization is ultimately responsible for the affairs of the organization – this book generally refers to the board when referring to the financial oversight body. The fact that it does so is not intended to imply that a finance committee is not necessary or helpful for any particular organization. Rather, reference to the board is a practical means of simplifying the text for the reader.*

Now more than ever before, nonprofit leaders must recognize the importance of risk management as an inherent part of organizational oversight and leadership. But what does proper risk management look like, and whose responsibility is it? Many nonprofit boards assume that the CEO and management have the "bases covered" and board involvement is often limited to reacting to flare-ups. Such an approach to risk management is problematic and dangerous for multiple reasons.

The members of management in a nonprofit organization are typically consumed with day-to-day operating activities and decisions – the "tyranny of the urgent." As a result, they frequently do not have or take the time to step back and proactively assess and address risks organization-wide. If that is the case, and the board is operating under the assumption that management "has it covered," the organization may be a ticking time-bomb for obvious reasons.

A COLLABORATIVE APPROACH INVOLVING BOTH THE BOARD AND MANAGEMENT

A key area of responsibility for the board is to ensure that the organization maintains an adequate approach to risk management. While the actual conduct of risk management activities is the responsibility of management under the authority of the CEO, the board should evaluate the organization's risk management strategy since the board has ultimate responsibility for oversight.

An effective risk management plan is a holistic one – one that addresses risk in all aspects of the organization's activities. The risk management plan should also be proactive rather than reactive – identifying risks before they become liabilities and taking appropriate steps to mitigate them.

ALL RISKS ARE FINANCIAL RISKS

All organizational risks carry a financial component. For example, the risk that an organization's building could be damaged by fire is both a physical risk and a financial risk. Noncompliance with applicable laws can also have financial implications. Even the risk of adverse public relations can have a financial impact – adverse public perception about an organization can negatively affect financial support by donors. Having an appropriate approach to overall risk management will help the board mitigate financial risks.

The board or its appropriate committee (see **Chapter 2**) should work with the CEO to ensure on an organization-wide basis that:

- Risks are identified and assessed as to likelihood of occurrence and severity;

- Risks are prioritized;

- Management has determined the extent to which identified risks have been mitigated; and

- Appropriate steps are taken to reduce identified risks to acceptable levels.

Reducing risk by implementing preventive measures is, of course, different from insuring against such risks. As part of its role in overseeing the adequacy of risk mitigation, the board should ensure that the organization maintains appropriate insurance coverage with respect to applicable risk areas.

AREAS OF RISK TO CONSIDER

In addressing the organization's overall risks, some *key* risk areas that warrant attention include, but are not limited to, the areas described below.

Each area of risk listed below is accompanied by a brief description and/or commentary. The description or commentary provided for each topic is not intended to be a thorough explanation – it is simply an overview in keeping with the purpose and scope of this book. Nonprofit board members are not expected to be experts in the areas described below, but they *are* expected to take reasonable and appropriate steps to ensure that the risk areas described below are satisfactorily addressed. Accomplishing that objective may involve engaging specialists in certain fields who can provide their expert commentary to the board and management in the appropriate areas. One way or another, the board should determine that the risk areas described below (and any others that are applicable) are addressed to their reasonable satisfaction.

CORPORATE STRUCTURE

Many nonprofit organizations operate within one legal entity – typically a not-for-profit corporation. That one corporation typically conducts all of the activities of the organization (including those that have more inherent risk than others) *and* owns all of the assets of the organization (real estate, investments, cash, etc.). In today's litigious society, a nonprofit organization that owns significant assets and that conducts risk-generating activities should consider whether a one-entity legal structure is appropriate for risk mitigation purposes. Utilization of a multiple-entity structure could potentially help an organization mitigate its financial risks – risks such as the loss of substantial assets due to an unreasonable or unfair "runaway jury" award in litigation that is not adequately covered by the organization's insurance policies.

The author, of course, does not advocate that any organization shirk its appropriate legal and financial liability. But whether the award determined by a court or jury is fair or appropriate can be an entirely different matter.

> *There is nothing unethical or improper about wisely structuring an organization's corporate structure to limit exposure to liability.*

For example, if (God forbid) something bad happens to a child while on a trip with an organization, is a liability of $10,000 reasonable? What about $1 million? Or what about $10 million? $50 million? In 2013, a student on a summer study trip with a Connecticut prep school was awarded $42 million by a jury in connection with a debilitating disease from a tick bite sustained during the trip. Whether the school had some legal responsibility and liability is one question. Whether that responsibility and liability should include a $42 million financial liability is a very different question. There is nothing unethical or improper about wisely structuring an organization's corporate structure to limit exposure to liability. An attorney on the finance committee of a nonprofit organization served by the author stated the he believed it might be negligent for an organization's leaders *not* to consider corporate structure as a prudent risk management strategy.

An organization wishing to avail itself of a multiple-entity structure should do so under the advice of excellent legal counsel and tax counsel with specific experience in this area. It is important to preserve tax exemptions (federal, state, and local) for the entities involved as part of a corporate structure modification, and the rules for doing so are highly technical.

Some attorneys take the position that a multiple-entity structure is not effective in limiting exposure of an organization's assets in the event of a liability claim that occurs in a related entity. The author has worked in this area extensively with organizations across the country, together with highly respected attorneys from multiple high-profile law firms. The vast majority of attorneys with whom the author has worked believe a multiple-entity structure can be an effective tool for risk mitigation when implemented properly. One attorney summed up his perspective noting that state laws allow corporations to have subsidiary corporations and limited liability companies for the *very purpose* of limiting liability. The author and his firm have provided tax counsel to numerous nonprofit organizations that have, under the advice of their legal counsel, adopted multiple-entity structures as part of an overall risk mitigation strategy.

No attorney will guarantee that a particular multiple-entity structure is "bullet-proof." But proper utilization of a multiple-entity structure may reduce an entity's exposure to loss in some situations. One prominent attorney described a multiple-entity structure as a "flying duck," which may be less prone to loss of assets than a "sitting duck."

> *One prominent attorney described a multiple-entity structure as a "flying duck," which may be less prone to loss of assets than a "sitting duck."*

FUNDRAISING PRACTICES

As a reputational matter, and to ensure compliance with the law, a nonprofit organization's fundraising practices should be conducted with integrity. Nonprofit organizations that engage in deceptive, misleading, or unethical fundraising practices damage the reputation of the organization, and can put the organization and its leaders in legal risk. Most states in the United States have laws and regulations governing charitable solicitations, and federal law can come into play as well. Of most fundamental importance, an organization should never solicit a contribution in a way that causes a donor to believe that funds will be used in a manner that is different from the manner in which they are actually used. The board should have a means of assessing the organization's fundraising practices. The author is aware of some nonprofit organizations that have their legal counsel review every proposed fundraising message prior to its distribution to ensure compliance with the law. While having legal counsel review every fundraising message may not be feasible for many organizations, the board should establish clear expectations for management regarding the integrity of the fundraising practices and should communicate with management about the organization's practices. The board should monitor the organization's fundraising activities and communications. Additionally, the board should be apprised of any complaints or investigations involving the organization's fundraising practices.

Tax Compliance

Compliance with applicable federal and other tax laws is a critical element of overall risk management. **Chapter 8** addresses the topic of tax compliance specifically.

General Legal Compliance

Compliance with applicable law is, of course, a fundamentally important element of risk management for a nonprofit organization. Areas of law for which noncompliance can have significant implications include, but are not limited to:

- Laws addressing the legal manner of governance of the organization

- Compliance with the organization's own governing documents (articles of incorporation and bylaws)

  - Compliance with key contractual agreements

  - Significant vendor contracts

  - Significant customer contracts

  - Significant loan agreements (including financial covenants)

- Human resources (labor, wage, healthcare, and employee benefits laws)

- Healthcare privacy laws

- Copyright law

- Laws governing the handling of donor-restricted funds

- Laws governing investment practices by nonprofit organizations

- Laws governing charitable solicitation

- Laws governing the reporting of actual or suspected child abuse

- Zoning and land use laws

- Laws governing nondiscrimination in public accommodations

- Building codes

Nonprofit organizations can assess their risks in these legal areas by consulting with legal experts specifically experienced in the applicable areas of law. Some law firms offer proactive assessment services sometimes referred to as "legal audits" that can help identify legal compliance issues that warrant attention.

CHILD MOLESTATION RISK

For organizations that serve children, child molestation risk warrants special attention due to the severity of the damages that can occur. In recent years, an increasing number of high-liability claims have been made against nonprofit organizations that serve children due to actual or alleged child molestation. Claims of that type can be devastating not only to the victims but also to an organization and its leadership, both reputationally and financially. Multiple Catholic dioceses in the United States have filed for bankruptcy protection in connection with child molestation claims and many other types of organizations have experienced major claims. The board of a nonprofit organization serving children should carefully evaluate the nature of the risks as well as prevention strategies and insurance coverage maintained by the organization. Published resources are available on this topic – particularly in the church arena. (See suggested reference at the end of this chapter.)

DATA SECURITY

Bad guys are continuously inventing new ways to attack and/or obtain sensitive data from people, government, businesses, and nonprofit organizations. As technological capabilities continue to increase, and we live in an increasingly connected world, every organization must consider the security of its sensitive data and employ reasonable steps to protect it. Failure to protect sensitive data can have legal, financial, and public relations ramifications and in extreme situations, can jeopardize an organization's ability to function. The board of a nonprofit organization should assess whether the organization's management is adequately addressing risks related to data security.

> *The board of a nonprofit organization should assess whether the organization's management is adequately addressing risks related to data security.*

INSURANCE COVERAGE

One significant aspect of risk management includes ensuring that the organization has appropriate insurance coverage for its significant risks. The evaluation of insurance coverage should include consultation with both legal counsel and highly experienced insurance agents. Specific coverage types to evaluate should include, but not be limited to:

- Property and casualty (for fire, theft, flood, vandalism, data loss, etc.);

- Business interruption;

- Data security, including cybersecurity;

- Employee theft;

- General liability;

- Sexual misconduct (including child molestation for organizations that serve children);

- Director and officer liability;

- Employment practices (for claims of discrimination, wrongful termination, sexual harassment, and other such matters related to employment practices);

- Fiduciary liability (for claims by employees related to the administration of employee benefit plans, particularly retirement plans); and

- "Key man" life or disability (for financial remuneration to the organization in the event of the death or disability of a key leader – useful where the organization could be adversely affected financially in the event of such an occurrence).

Organization leaders should discuss with their legal counsel and insurance agents whether they have risk exposures that may warrant other types of coverage.

INTERNAL FINANCIAL CONTROLS

A fundamental element of financial risk management involves ensuring that the organization has an adequate and appropriate internal control structure in place with respect to financial activities. A detailed description of the topic of internal control is outside the scope of this book. For more specific guidance in this area, nonprofit organizations may find the book *Church Finance* helpful, co-written by the author of this book and published by Christianity Today. Notwithstanding its title, the principles of internal control described in *Church Finance* are generally applicable to a wide variety of nonprofit organizations.

While management of the organization is responsible for establishing and maintaining an appropriate system of internal control, the board is responsible for overseeing management's efforts in this regard. The board should request that management periodically articulate to the board the methods and practices employed by management to ensure that the system of internal control is adequate. The most common way that boards independently address their responsibilities in this area is through the organization's relationship with its independent auditing firm. For organizations that have annual independent audits of their financial statements, in selecting the independent CPA firm to perform the audits, the board should clearly and specifically address the topic of internal control. There are *very, very* dramatic differences among CPA firms in the manner, extent, breadth, and depth with which they assess internal control as part of an audit engagement. The board should ensure that the firm it engages is highly experienced in the arena of nonprofit organizations, and should obtain a clear and specific understanding of the manner in which the firm addresses internal control. One of the most valuable outcomes of a well-performed independent audit is a report to management and the board addressing internal control recommendations identified during the audit.

Knowing that the CPA firm has looked extensively at the organization's internal controls – especially those related to cash transactions – can help the board have more confidence in the organization's systems.

The report issued by a CPA firm on internal control in connection with the audit of the organization's financial statements is not an opinion on internal control. Rather, it is a report with recommendations to address weaknesses and vulnerabilities identified in the audit. An opinion on internal control is a much more extensive (and expensive) engagement. Engaging a CPA firm to render an opinion with respect to an organization's internal control systems is rare in the nonprofit sector.

Very large nonprofit organizations sometimes engage the services of internal auditors to assist the board (and/or its committees) in addressing internal control and other risk and compliance matters. (See **Chapter 3** for more information about internal audits.)

Below are some very basic observations about the critically important area of internal control.

Key Principles of Internal Control for Cash Transactions

Specific internal controls related to cash transactions should be developed and maintained based on certain key principles. Three primary applicable principles are:

- Segregation of duties,

- Dual control, and

- Appropriate oversight and monitoring.

SEGREGATION OF DUTIES

Certain duties with respect to cash transactions and related activities are not compatible and should not be carried out by one person or by related persons. A lack of appropriate segregation of duties creates an environment in which there is a greater risk that misappropriation, embezzlement, or fraud could occur and not be detected in a timely manner.

As a general rule, it is important to separate duties that involve the following roles with respect to cash:

- Custody or control over cash and investments (including the authority to make disbursements) and

- Accounting responsibilities.

DUAL CONTROL

The practice of dual control relates to having "live" funds (funds received by the organization that have not been fully processed, recorded, and deposited in the bank) in the custody of at least two unrelated people working together at all times. A lack of dual control in circumstances where it is warranted creates an environment in which there is a greater risk that misappropriation, embezzlement, or fraud could occur and not be detected in a timely manner.

APPROPRIATE OVERSIGHT AND MONITORING

In addition to the principles of segregation of duties and dual control, nonprofit leaders must engage in adequate oversight and monitoring of the organization's financial affairs. That includes carefully reviewing financial reports, reconciliations, and other records. This responsibility also includes monitoring to verify that policies, procedures, and internal controls which are supposed to be in place are, indeed, in place and being carried out by those who are responsible.

There are many more important and specific elements of internal control to be considered by any organization in addition to the very basic principles described above. As mentioned above, the board should have a means for satisfying itself that this important aspect of the organization's operations is addressed adequately.

PHYSICAL SAFETY

A risk area of much more prominence today than in the past is that of physical safety. Physical safety risks can arise in many ways, including safety hazards in an organization's facilities, transportation, and even violent confrontations (workplace violence, active shooters, etc.). An organization's board should work with the CEO of the organization to ensure that the organization has identified what it believes to be its significant risks in the area of physical safety and that it has implemented appropriate and reasonable safeguards to mitigate those risks where feasible. Since physical safety risks can take so many different forms, an organization should consider engaging the services of experts to assist them in addressing particular risk areas. For example, a school may wish to engage the services of local law enforcement authorities, or even a specialized consultant, with respect to the matter of campus safety. An organization with significant transportation activities may wish to engage a transportation safety consultant. Engaging and relying on the advice of experts in particularly high-risk areas can not only reduce the organization's physical safety risks, but can also help the organization mount a legal defense in the event it is sued by a plaintiff claiming that the organization was negligent.

LEADERSHIP SUCCESSION

Many well-run and well-governed nonprofit organizations suffer missionally and financially when a talented and charismatic leader retires or otherwise leaves the employment of the organization. When such a departure comes suddenly and unexpectedly, the impact can be particularly severe. The topic of leadership succession can be uncomfortable for boards to discuss. As with the topic of estate planning, many people simply don't like thinking about or discussing what will happen when they are no longer around. The same can be true when discussing the ultimate departure of a CEO from a nonprofit organization. However, an organization's board must realize that, in many cases, the departure of a gifted leader with no succession plan creates a significant risk for the organization – a risk that warrants attention.

Adequately addressing the issue of leadership succession does not necessarily mean picking the next CEO of the organization. A solid leadership succession plan may include designating with clarity who would serve as the acting CEO in the event of the sudden and unexpected departure by the existing CEO, together with a specific plan for *how* the next CEO will be selected. Having a temporary contingent leadership plan in place, together with a well-thought-out *process* for selecting the next CEO may be all that is needed. Without such measures in place, the departure of a CEO can result in a period of confusion

– and even heated disagreement – among board members and others at a time when the organization is in a very vulnerable state. And it can significantly extend the amount of time required to identify and employ the next CEO. Good planning by the board can prevent such a result.

PUBLIC RELATIONS

Controversial, adverse, high-profile publicity can be an unexpected and unwelcome guest for any organization. Sometimes, a bad situation becomes worse for an organization because of how it is handled. When an organization finds itself having to deal with adverse publicity, handling it properly is critical.

Imagine a tragedy of a child being severely injured in a school bus accident. The media pounces, seeking commentary from anyone who will comment. A television news station interviews a teacher in the school who has no role whatsoever with respect to the bus operations. The teacher states that she has heard that there were some safety concerns about some of the buses, but doesn't know whether that had a role in the tragedy that occurred. That teacher's comments become a featured part of the news story broadcast about the incident.

Clearly, in the example described in the preceding paragraph, the teacher interviewed should not be making stray comments about which he or she has no direct knowledge and which could be damaging to the school. The risk of such stray commentary can be reduced significantly by implementation of an appropriate media communications / public relations policy. Such a policy should clearly state who in the organization is authorized to speak to the media on behalf of the organization and should prohibit others from doing so. The policy should be well-known to the organization's employees.

Additionally, when and if a crisis occurs, an organization may benefit significantly from the counsel of a public relations firm. It can be an added element of stress for the organization to have to identify and hire such a firm in the middle of a crisis. If the organization can *proactively* identify and establish a relationship with a public relations firm with which it is comfortable, that firm can jump right in to help in the unfortunate event that a crisis warrants public relations assistance.

———————————— -   - ————————————

ADDITIONAL RESOURCES FOR ADDRESSING RISK MANAGEMENT

Some additional sources of information that may be helpful to organizations addressing overall risk management include:

NONPROFIT RISK MANAGEMENT CENTER
(www.nonprofitrisk.org)

REDUCING THE RISK (CHILD SAFETY RESOURCES)
(www.reducingtherisk.com)

Appendix A

ANNUAL FINANCIAL OVERSIGHT CHECKLIST FOR BOARDS AND FINANCE COMMITTEES

*Given the fact that an organization may decide, as described in **Chapter 2**, not to utilize a finance committee or its equivalent – and the reality that even if a finance committee is utilized, the governing body (board) of the organization is ultimately responsible for the affairs of the organization – this book generally refers to the board when referring to the financial oversight body. The fact that it does so is not intended to imply that a finance committee is not necessary or helpful for any particular organization. Rather, reference to the board is a practical means of simplifying the text for the reader.*

Annual Checklist

At least once a year, the board should determine that the following matters have been addressed satisfactorily to the extent they apply to their organization. The items below are arranged according to the chapters of the book for ease of reference.

CHAPTER 1

1. Are all board members aware of their fiduciary duties with respect to overall oversight and financial oversight of the organization as described in **Chapter 1**?

   Has this item been addressed satisfactorily within the last 12 months?

   ☐ Yes   ☐ No   ☐ *N/A - if not applicable explain why.*

   How was it addressed?

   By whom was it addressed?

   When was it addressed?

   Person affirming completion of this item and date completed.

   _____   _____

   Name   Date

CHAPTER 2

2. Has the board determined, using an appropriate framework, what committees (if any) are needed to assist the board in performing board-level work?

Has this item been addressed satisfactorily within the last 12 months?

☐ Yes   ☐ No   ☐ *N/A - if not applicable explain why.*

How was it addressed?

By whom was it addressed?

When was it addressed?

Person affirming completion of this item and date completed.

_____   _____
         Name   Date

a. Does each ad hoc committee addressing financial matters have a clear board-level purpose and assignment? (This principle applies to all ad hoc committees, but this checklist question is limited to financial matters given the scope of this book.)

Has this item been addressed satisfactorily within the last 12 months?

☐ Yes   ☐ No   ☐ *N/A - if not applicable explain why.*

How was it addressed?

By whom was it addressed?

When was it addressed?

Person affirming completion of this item and date completed.

_____   _____
         Name   Date

b. If a finance committee is utilized, does the committee have an appropriate charter in place as described in **Chapter 2** and does it follow its charter? (This principle applies to all committees, but this checklist question is limited to the finance committee given the scope of this book.)

Has this item been addressed satisfactorily within the last 12 months?

☐ Yes   ☐ No   ☐ *N/A - if not applicable explain why.*

How was it addressed?

By whom was it addressed?

When was it addressed?

Person affirming completion of this item and date completed.

_____   _____
Name   Date

c. Are committees charged with overseeing financial matters performing board-level work and not intervening in operational matters? (This principle applies to all committees, but this checklist question is limited to financial matters given the scope of this book.)

Has this item been addressed satisfactorily within the last 12 months?

☐ Yes   ☐ No   ☐ *N/A - if not applicable explain why.*

How was it addressed?

By whom was it addressed?

When was it addressed?

Person affirming completion of this item and date completed.

_____   _____
Name   Date

CHAPTER 3

3. Does the organization employ audit or other financial accountability measures appropriate for the size, nature, and scope of its activities as described in **Chapter 3**?

   Has this item been addressed satisfactorily within the last 12 months?

   ☐ Yes   ☐ No   ☐ *N/A - if not applicable explain why.*

   How was it addressed?

   By whom was it addressed?

   When was it addressed?

   Person affirming completion of this item and date completed.

   _____   _____
            Name   Date

4. If an external audit is performed, has the organization engaged a CPA firm to perform the audit that is highly-experienced in serving nonprofit organizations and that has the expertise to proactively address the organization's internal control and tax compliance?

   Has this item been addressed satisfactorily within the last 12 months?

   ☐ Yes   ☐ No   ☐ *N/A - if not applicable explain why.*

   How was it addressed?

   By whom was it addressed?

   When was it addressed?

   Person affirming completion of this item and date completed.

   _____   _____
            Name   Date

5. If an audit committee is utilized, does the committee have an appropriate charter in place as described in **Chapter 3** and does it follow its charter?

   Has this item been addressed satisfactorily within the last 12 months?

   ☐ Yes   ☐ No   ☐ *N/A - if not applicable explain why.*

   How was it addressed?

   By whom was it addressed?

   When was it addressed?

   Person affirming completion of this item and date completed.

   _____   _____
   Name   Date

6. If the organization utilizes an internal audit process, are the guidelines set forth in **Chapter 3** for internal audit activities being followed?

   Has this item been addressed satisfactorily within the last 12 months?

   ☐ Yes   ☐ No   ☐ *N/A - if not applicable explain why.*

   How was it addressed?

   By whom was it addressed?

   When was it addressed?

   Person affirming completion of this item and date completed.

   _____   _____
   Name   Date

CHAPTER 5 (CHAPTER 4 OMITTED FROM THIS LIST INTENTIONALLY)

7. Has the organization had appropriately experienced legal counsel review its articles of incorporation, bylaws, and board-approved policies within the last three years?

Has this item been addressed satisfactorily within the last 12 months?

☐ Yes   ☐ No   ☐ *N/A - if not applicable explain why.*

How was it addressed?

By whom was it addressed?

When was it addressed?

Person affirming completion of this item and date completed.

_____   _____
         Name   Date

8. Did the board have appropriately experienced legal counsel review and/or assist in drafting any amendments to the articles of incorporation, bylaws, or board-approved policies?

Has this item been addressed satisfactorily within the last 12 months?

☐ Yes   ☐ No   ☐ *N/A - if not applicable explain why.*

How was it addressed?

By whom was it addressed?

When was it addressed?

Person affirming completion of this item and date completed.

_____   _____
         Name   Date

9. Is the organization operating in compliance with its articles of incorporation, bylaws, and board-approved policies?

Has this item been addressed satisfactorily within the last 12 months?

☐ Yes ☐ No ☐ *N/A - if not applicable explain why.*

How was it addressed?

By whom was it addressed?

When was it addressed?

Person affirming completion of this item and date completed.

Name	Date

10. Has the board evaluated, within the last year, whether it has appropriate policies in place, taking into consideration the list of policies described in **Chapter 5** and other relevant factors?

Has this item been addressed satisfactorily within the last 12 months?

☐ Yes ☐ No ☐ *N/A - if not applicable explain why.*

How was it addressed?

By whom was it addressed?

When was it addressed?

Person affirming completion of this item and date completed.

Name	Date

CHAPTER 6

11. Is the financial reporting process one that provides the board with accurate, relevant, and timely information in a format easily understood by the board and usable by the board in carrying out its financial oversight responsibilities?

Has this item been addressed satisfactorily within the last 12 months?

☐ Yes   ☐ No   ☐ *N/A - if not applicable explain why.*

How was it addressed?

By whom was it addressed?

When was it addressed?

Person affirming completion of this item and date completed.

_____   _____
Name   Date

12. Does the board drive the process of determining the nature, scope, and format of financial information provided to the board?

Has this item been addressed satisfactorily within the last 12 months?

☐ Yes   ☐ No   ☐ *N/A - if not applicable explain why.*

How was it addressed?

By whom was it addressed?

When was it addressed?

Person affirming completion of this item and date completed.

_____   _____
Name   Date

13. Has the board developed a list of "key questions" for which it needs appropriate responses on an ongoing, periodic basis?

Has this item been addressed satisfactorily within the last 12 months?

☐ Yes   ☐ No   ☐ *N/A - if not applicable explain why.*

How was it addressed?

By whom was it addressed?

When was it addressed?

Person affirming completion of this item and date completed.

_____   _____
Name   Date

a. Has the board considered the example questions illustrated in **Chapter 6**?

Has this item been addressed satisfactorily within the last 12 months?

☐ Yes   ☐ No   ☐ *N/A - if not applicable explain why.*

How was it addressed?

By whom was it addressed?

When was it addressed?

Person affirming completion of this item and date completed.

_____   _____
Name   Date

b. Does the nature, scope, and format of the financial information provided to the board provide adequate and timely answers to those specific questions?

Has this item been addressed satisfactorily within the last 12 months?

☐ Yes   ☐ No   ☐ *N/A - if not applicable explain why.*

How was it addressed?

By whom was it addressed?

When was it addressed?

Person affirming completion of this item and date completed.

_____   _____
Name   Date

CHAPTER 7

14. Has the board specifically evaluated the organization's financial health as described in **Chapter 7** and appropriately addressed any concerns?

Has this item been addressed satisfactorily within the last 12 months?

☐ Yes   ☐ No   ☐ *N/A - if not applicable explain why.*

How was it addressed?

By whom was it addressed?

When was it addressed?

Person affirming completion of this item and date completed.

_____   _____
Name   Date

15. Does the organization have specific metrics or targets for its financial health, including targets for liquidity and financial position?

Has this item been addressed satisfactorily within the last 12 months?

☐ Yes ☐ No ☐ *N/A - if not applicable explain why.*

How was it addressed?

By whom was it addressed?

When was it addressed?

Person affirming completion of this item and date completed.

Name	Date

a. Is there a specific action plan to achieve or maintain those targets?

Has this item been addressed satisfactorily within the last 12 months?

☐ Yes ☐ No ☐ *N/A - if not applicable explain why.*

How was it addressed?

By whom was it addressed?

When was it addressed?

Person affirming completion of this item and date completed.

Name	Date

b. Has the board considered the metrics suggested in **Chapter 7**?

Has this item been addressed satisfactorily within the last 12 months?

☐ Yes   ☐ No   ☐ *N/A - if not applicable explain why.*

How was it addressed?

By whom was it addressed?

When was it addressed?

Person affirming completion of this item and date completed.

_____	_____
Name	Date

16. If the organization has a significant investment portfolio, does it have an appropriate investment policy in place, and is the policy being followed?

Has this item been addressed satisfactorily within the last 12 months?

☐ Yes   ☐ No   ☐ *N/A - if not applicable explain why.*

How was it addressed?

By whom was it addressed?

When was it addressed?

Person affirming completion of this item and date completed.

_____	_____
Name	Date

17. Has the board determined whether the organization is impacted by any charity ratings organizations or watchdog groups?

Has this item been addressed satisfactorily within the last 12 months?

☐ Yes   ☐ No   ☐ *N/A - if not applicable explain why.*

How was it addressed?

By whom was it addressed?

When was it addressed?

Person affirming completion of this item and date completed.

_____   _____
Name   Date

a. If the organization is impacted by any such groups, does the board have an understanding of how the organization is rated or portrayed by such groups and the effects of such ratings or portrayals?

Has this item been addressed satisfactorily within the last 12 months?

☐ Yes   ☐ No   ☐ *N/A - if not applicable explain why.*

How was it addressed?

By whom was it addressed?

When was it addressed?

Person affirming completion of this item and date completed.

_____   _____
Name   Date

i. If warranted, has the board provided management with direction or expectations regarding the organization's ratings or portrayals by such groups?

Has this item been addressed satisfactorily within the last 12 months?

☐ Yes   ☐ No   ☐ *N/A - if not applicable explain why.*

How was it addressed?

By whom was it addressed?

When was it addressed?

Person affirming completion of this item and date completed.

Name	Date

CHAPTER 8

18. In order to address the organization's compliance with applicable tax laws, does the board do the following:

a. Engage the services of a CPA firm highly experienced in tax compliance matters for nonprofit, tax-exempt organizations?

Has this item been addressed satisfactorily within the last 12 months?

☐ Yes   ☐ No   ☐ *N/A - if not applicable explain why.*

How was it addressed?

By whom was it addressed?

When was it addressed?

Person affirming completion of this item and date completed.

Name	Date

b. Ensure that the specific members of the CPA firm assigned to the organization are, themselves, highly experienced in such matters?

Has this item been addressed satisfactorily within the last 12 months?

☐ Yes   ☐ No   ☐ *N/A - if not applicable explain why.*

How was it addressed?

By whom was it addressed?

When was it addressed?

Person affirming completion of this item and date completed.

Name   Date

c. Have a clear understanding with the CPA firm that the firm is expected to *proactively* help the organization maintain its tax compliance, and not simply be *reactive* to issues or questions raised by the organization?

Has this item been addressed satisfactorily within the last 12 months?

☐ Yes   ☐ No   ☐ *N/A - if not applicable explain why.*

How was it addressed?

By whom was it addressed?

When was it addressed?

Person affirming completion of this item and date completed.

Name   Date

19. Has the board specifically addressed to its satisfaction compliance in the key areas described in **Chapter 8**:

   a. Executive compensation-setting?

   Has this item been addressed satisfactorily within the last 12 months?

   ☐ Yes   ☐ No   ☐ *N/A - if not applicable explain why.*

   How was it addressed?

   By whom was it addressed?

   When was it addressed?

   Person affirming completion of this item and date completed.

   _____   _____

          Name   Date

   b. Related party transactions?

   Has this item been addressed satisfactorily within the last 12 months?

   ☐ Yes   ☐ No   ☐ *N/A - if not applicable explain why.*

   How was it addressed?

   By whom was it addressed?

   When was it addressed?

   Person affirming completion of this item and date completed.

   _____   _____

          Name   Date

c. Payroll tax withholding and remittance?

Has this item been addressed satisfactorily within the last 12 months?

☐ Yes ☐ No ☐ *N/A - if not applicable explain why.*

How was it addressed?

By whom was it addressed?

When was it addressed?

Person affirming completion of this item and date completed.

Name	Date

d. IRS Form 990?

Has this item been addressed satisfactorily within the last 12 months?

☐ Yes ☐ No ☐ *N/A - if not applicable explain why.*

How was it addressed?

By whom was it addressed?

When was it addressed?

Person affirming completion of this item and date completed.

Name	Date

CHAPTER 9

20. Does the organization have an adequate, proactive, organization-wide process in place, as described in **Chapter 9**, to identify, evaluate, and respond to risks facing the organization?

    Has this item been addressed satisfactorily within the last 12 months?

    ☐ Yes   ☐ No   ☐ *N/A - if not applicable explain why.*

    How was it addressed?

    By whom was it addressed?

    When was it addressed?

    Person affirming completion of this item and date completed.

    _____   _____
    Name   Date

21. Has the board addressed to its satisfaction, with the assistance of legal counsel and subject matter experts as necessary, possible risks in each of the following areas:

    a. Corporate structure?

       Has this item been addressed satisfactorily within the last 12 months?

       ☐ Yes   ☐ No   ☐ *N/A - if not applicable explain why.*

       How was it addressed?

       By whom was it addressed?

       When was it addressed?

       Person affirming completion of this item and date completed.

       _____   _____
       Name   Date

b. Fundraising practices?

Has this item been addressed satisfactorily within the last 12 months?

☐ Yes ☐ No ☐ *N/A - if not applicable explain why.*

How was it addressed?

By whom was it addressed?

When was it addressed?

Person affirming completion of this item and date completed.

_____ _____
Name   Date

c. General legal compliance:
   i. Laws addressing the legal manner of governance of the organization?

   Has this item been addressed satisfactorily within the last 12 months?

   ☐ Yes ☐ No ☐ *N/A - if not applicable explain why.*

   How was it addressed?

   By whom was it addressed?

   When was it addressed?

   Person affirming completion of this item and date completed.

   _____ _____
   Name   Date

ii. Compliance with the organization's own governing documents (articles of incorporation and bylaws)?

Has this item been addressed satisfactorily within the last 12 months?

☐ Yes   ☐ No   ☐ *N/A - if not applicable explain why.*

How was it addressed?

By whom was it addressed?

When was it addressed?

Person affirming completion of this item and date completed.

Name	Date

iii. Compliance with key contractual agreements:

1. Significant vendor contracts?

Has this item been addressed satisfactorily within the last 12 months?

☐ Yes   ☐ No   ☐ *N/A - if not applicable explain why.*

How was it addressed?

By whom was it addressed?

When was it addressed?

Person affirming completion of this item and date completed.

Name	Date

2. Significant customer contracts?

Has this item been addressed satisfactorily within the last 12 months?

☐ Yes ☐ No ☐ *N/A - if not applicable explain why.*

How was it addressed?

By whom was it addressed?

When was it addressed?

Person affirming completion of this item and date completed.

_____   _____
Name   Date

3. Significant loan agreements (including financial covenants)?

Has this item been addressed satisfactorily within the last 12 months?

☐ Yes ☐ No ☐ *N/A - if not applicable explain why.*

How was it addressed?

By whom was it addressed?

When was it addressed?

Person affirming completion of this item and date completed.

_____   _____
Name   Date

iv. Human resources (labor, wage, healthcare, and employee benefits laws)?

Has this item been addressed satisfactorily within the last 12 months?

☐ Yes   ☐ No   ☐ *N/A - if not applicable explain why.*

How was it addressed?

By whom was it addressed?

When was it addressed?

Person affirming completion of this item and date completed.

Name	Date

v. Healthcare privacy laws?

Has this item been addressed satisfactorily within the last 12 months?

☐ Yes   ☐ No   ☐ *N/A - if not applicable explain why.*

How was it addressed?

By whom was it addressed?

When was it addressed?

Person affirming completion of this item and date completed.

Name	Date

vi. Copyright law?

Has this item been addressed satisfactorily within the last 12 months?

☐ Yes   ☐ No   ☐ *N/A - if not applicable explain why.*

How was it addressed?

By whom was it addressed?

When was it addressed?

Person affirming completion of this item and date completed.

_____   _____
Name   Date

vii. Laws governing the handling of donor-restricted funds?

Has this item been addressed satisfactorily within the last 12 months?

☐ Yes   ☐ No   ☐ *N/A - if not applicable explain why.*

How was it addressed?

By whom was it addressed?

When was it addressed?

Person affirming completion of this item and date completed.

_____   _____
Name   Date

viii. Laws governing investment practices by nonprofit organizations?

Has this item been addressed satisfactorily within the last 12 months?

☐ Yes ☐ No ☐ *N/A - if not applicable explain why.*

How was it addressed?

By whom was it addressed?

When was it addressed?

Person affirming completion of this item and date completed.

_____ _____
Name   Date

ix. Laws governing charitable solicitation?

Has this item been addressed satisfactorily within the last 12 months?

☐ Yes ☐ No ☐ *N/A - if not applicable explain why.*

How was it addressed?

By whom was it addressed?

When was it addressed?

Person affirming completion of this item and date completed.

_____ _____
Name   Date

x. Laws governing the reporting of actual or suspected child abuse?

Has this item been addressed satisfactorily within the last 12 months?

☐ Yes   ☐ No   ☐ *N/A - if not applicable explain why.*

How was it addressed?

By whom was it addressed?

When was it addressed?

Person affirming completion of this item and date completed.

_____   _____
        Name   Date

xi. Zoning and land use laws?

Has this item been addressed satisfactorily within the last 12 months?

☐ Yes   ☐ No   ☐ *N/A - if not applicable explain why.*

How was it addressed?

By whom was it addressed?

When was it addressed?

Person affirming completion of this item and date completed.

_____   _____
        Name   Date

xii. Laws   governing   nondiscrimination   in   public accommodations?

Has this item been addressed satisfactorily within the last 12 months?

☐ Yes   ☐ No   ☐ *N/A - if not applicable explain why.*

How was it addressed?

By whom was it addressed?

When was it addressed?

Person affirming completion of this item and date completed.

Name	Date

xiii. Building codes?

Has this item been addressed satisfactorily within the last 12 months?

☐ Yes   ☐ No   ☐ *N/A - if not applicable explain why.*

How was it addressed?

By whom was it addressed?

When was it addressed?

Person affirming completion of this item and date completed.

Name	Date

xiv. Other areas of law identified by the board and its legal counsel?

Has this item been addressed satisfactorily within the last 12 months?

☐ Yes ☐ No ☐ *N/A - if not applicable explain why.*

How was it addressed?

By whom was it addressed?

When was it addressed?

Person affirming completion of this item and date completed.

_____   _____
Name   Date

22. If the organization serves or accommodates children, has the board determined, in working with the CEO, that the organization has appropriate safeguards in place to reduce the risk of child molestation?

Has this item been addressed satisfactorily within the last 12 months?

☐ Yes ☐ No ☐ *N/A - if not applicable explain why.*

How was it addressed?

By whom was it addressed?

When was it addressed?

Person affirming completion of this item and date completed.

_____   _____
Name   Date

23. Has the board, in working with management, determined that appropriate and adequate insurance coverages are in place:

a. Property and casualty (for fire, theft, flood, vandalism, data loss, etc.)?

Has this item been addressed satisfactorily within the last 12 months?

☐ Yes   ☐ No   ☐ *N/A - if not applicable explain why.*

How was it addressed?

By whom was it addressed?

When was it addressed?

Person affirming completion of this item and date completed.

_____   _____
         Name   Date

b. Business interruption?

Has this item been addressed satisfactorily within the last 12 months?

☐ Yes   ☐ No   ☐ *N/A - if not applicable explain why.*

How was it addressed?

By whom was it addressed?

When was it addressed?

Person affirming completion of this item and date completed.

_____   _____
         Name   Date

c. Data security, including cybersecurity?

Has this item been addressed satisfactorily within the last 12 months?

☐ Yes ☐ No ☐ *N/A - if not applicable explain why.*

How was it addressed?

By whom was it addressed?

When was it addressed?

Person affirming completion of this item and date completed.

_____ _____
Name Date

d. Employee theft?

Has this item been addressed satisfactorily within the last 12 months?

☐ Yes ☐ No ☐ *N/A - if not applicable explain why.*

How was it addressed?

By whom was it addressed?

When was it addressed?

Person affirming completion of this item and date completed.

_____ _____
Name Date

e. General liability?

Has this item been addressed satisfactorily within the last 12 months?

☐ Yes   ☐ No   ☐ *N/A - if not applicable explain why.*

How was it addressed?

By whom was it addressed?

When was it addressed?

Person affirming completion of this item and date completed.

_____	_____
Name	Date

f. Sexual misconduct (including child molestation for organizations that serve children)?

Has this item been addressed satisfactorily within the last 12 months?

☐ Yes   ☐ No   ☐ *N/A - if not applicable explain why.*

How was it addressed?

By whom was it addressed?

When was it addressed?

Person affirming completion of this item and date completed.

_____	_____
Name	Date

g. Director and officer liability?

Has this item been addressed satisfactorily within the last 12 months?

☐ Yes ☐ No ☐ *N/A - if not applicable explain why.*

How was it addressed?

By whom was it addressed?

When was it addressed?

Person affirming completion of this item and date completed.

_____ _____
Name Date

h. Employment practices (for claims of discrimination, wrongful termination, sexual harassment, and other such matters related to employment practices)?

Has this item been addressed satisfactorily within the last 12 months?

☐ Yes ☐ No ☐ *N/A - if not applicable explain why.*

How was it addressed?

By whom was it addressed?

When was it addressed?

Person affirming completion of this item and date completed.

_____ _____
Name Date

i. Fiduciary liability (for claims by employees related to the administration of employee benefit plans, particularly retirement plans)?

Has this item been addressed satisfactorily within the last 12 months?

☐ Yes   ☐ No   ☐ *N/A - if not applicable explain why.*

How was it addressed?

By whom was it addressed?

When was it addressed?

Person affirming completion of this item and date completed.

               Name   Date

j. "Key man" life or disability (for financial remuneration to the organization in the event of the death or disability of a key leader – useful where the organization could be adversely affected financially in the event of such an occurrence)?

Has this item been addressed satisfactorily within the last 12 months?

☐ Yes   ☐ No   ☐ *N/A - if not applicable explain why.*

How was it addressed?

By whom was it addressed?

When was it addressed?

Person affirming completion of this item and date completed.

               Name   Date

k. Other coverage areas identified by the board, under the advice of the organization's legal counsel and insurance agents?

Has this item been addressed satisfactorily within the last 12 months?

☐ Yes ☐ No ☐ *N/A - if not applicable explain why.*

How was it addressed?

By whom was it addressed?

When was it addressed?

Person affirming completion of this item and date completed.

_____   _____
        Name   Date

24. Has the board determined to its satisfaction, as described in **Chapter 9**, that the organization has implemented appropriate internal financial controls to safeguard the organization's assets and to reduce the risk of fraud, theft, misappropriation, misstatements in financial reporting, and other financial improprieties?

Has this item been addressed satisfactorily within the last 12 months?

☐ Yes ☐ No ☐ *N/A - if not applicable explain why.*

How was it addressed?

By whom was it addressed?

When was it addressed?

Person affirming completion of this item and date completed.

_____   _____
        Name   Date

25. Has the board addressed to its satisfaction, as described in **Chapter 9**, risks related to physical safety in the organization's operations?

Has this item been addressed satisfactorily within the last 12 months?

☐ Yes   ☐ No   ☐ *N/A - if not applicable explain why.*

How was it addressed?

By whom was it addressed?

When was it addressed?

Person affirming completion of this item and date completed.

_____   _____
            Name   Date

26. Has the board addressed to its satisfaction, as described in **Chapter 9**, risks related to leadership succession?

Has this item been addressed satisfactorily within the last 12 months?

☐ Yes   ☐ No   ☐ *N/A - if not applicable explain why.*

How was it addressed?

By whom was it addressed?

When was it addressed?

Person affirming completion of this item and date completed.

_____   _____
            Name   Date

27. Does the organization have an appropriate approach to public relations, and does it have a relationship with a public relations firm to assist in the event of sudden and unexpected adverse publicity, as described in **Chapter 9**?

Has this item been addressed satisfactorily within the last 12 months?

☐ Yes ☐ No ☐ *N/A - if not applicable explain why.*

How was it addressed?

By whom was it addressed?

When was it addressed?

Person affirming completion of this item and date completed.

Name	Date

Appendix B

--- - - ---

SAMPLE CONFLICTS-OF-INTEREST POLICY

As with any significant policy, an organization should consult with legal counsel in adopting a policy covering the topics addressed herein.

1. <u>Purpose</u>. The purpose of the conflicts-of-interest policy is to protect the Corporation's interest when it is contemplating entering into a transaction or arrangement that might benefit the private interests of certain persons covered by the Policy. This policy is intended to supplement, but not replace, any applicable state laws governing conflicts of interest applicable to nonprofit corporations.

2. <u>Definitions</u>.

    (a) <u>Interested Person</u>.

    (1) <u>General Rule</u>. Any person who is a "disqualified person" within the meaning of Treas. Reg. §53.4958-3 is an "interested person" for purposes of this policy. Thus, any person who is, or during the preceding 5 years was, in a position to exercise substantial influence over the affairs of the Corporation is an "interested person." If an individual or entity is an interested person with respect to the Corporation or any entity affiliated with the Corporation, he or she is an interested person with respect to all affiliated entities.

    (2) <u>Particular persons</u>. Any person who is, or who was during the past 5 years, a director, principal officer, or member of a committee with board delegated powers, and who has a direct or indirect financial interest, as defined below, is an "interested person." In addition, the spouse, ancestors, siblings, and descendants (and spouse of any ancestor, sibling, or descendant) of any such person is an interested party. Finally, any business, trust, or estate, at

139

least 35% of which is owned by one or more interested persons, is itself an interested person. Other factors, e.g., being the founder of the Corporation, a substantial contributor to the Corporation, or a key executive who is not an officer, will also be taken into account in determining whether an individual or entity is an interested person.

(b) Financial Interest. A person has a financial interest if the person has, directly or indirectly, through business, investment or family-

   (1) an ownership or investment interest in any entity with which the Corporation has a transaction or arrangement;

   (2) a compensation arrangement with the Corporation or with any entity or individual with which the Corporation has a transaction or arrangement; or

   (3) a potential ownership or investment interest in, or compensation arran¬gement with, any entity or individual with which the Corporation is negotiating a transaction or arrangement.

(c) Compensation includes direct and indirect remuneration, as well as gifts or favors that are substantial in nature.

3. Procedures.

   (a) Duty to Disclose. In connection with any actual or possible conflict of interest, an interested person must disclose the existence and nature of his or her financial interest, and must be given the opportunity to disclose all material facts, to the directors and members of committees with board delegated powers that are considering the proposed transaction or arrangement.

   (b) Determining whether a conflict of interest exists. After disclosure of the financial interest and all material facts, and after any discussion with the interested person, he/she shall leave the governing board or committee meeting while the determination of a conflict of interest is discussed and voted upon. The remaining board or committee members shall decide if a conflict of interest exists.

(c) Procedures for Addressing the Conflict of Interest.

(1) An interested person may make a presentation at the board or committee meeting, but after the presentation, he or she shall leave the meeting during the discussion of and the vote on the transaction or arrangement that results in the conflict of interest.

(2) The chairperson of the board or committee shall, if appropriate, appoint a disinterested person or committee to investigate alternatives to the proposed transaction or arrangement.

(3) After exercising due diligence, the board or committee shall determine whether the Corporation can obtain a more advantageous transaction or arrangement with reasonable efforts from a person or entity that would not give rise to a conflict of interest.

(4) If a more advantageous transaction or arrangement is not reasonably attainable under circumstances that would not give rise to a conflict of interest, the board or committee shall determine by a majority vote of the disinterested directors or committee members whether the transaction or arrangement is in the Corporation's best interest and for its own benefit, and whether the transaction is fair and reasonable to the Corporation. The board or committee shall make its decision as to whether to enter into the transaction or arrangement in conformity with such determination.

(5) Each agreement with an interested person shall contain an appropriate provision permitting the agreement to be modified or terminated in the event that the Internal Revenue Service determines that any transaction that is the subject of the agreement is an excess benefit transaction within the meaning of §4958 of the Internal Revenue Code.

(6) For purposes of this policy, a disinterested person is one who is not an interested person with respect to the transaction, who is not in an employment or other financial relationship with any disqualified person with respect to the transaction, and who does not have any other material financial interest that may be affected by the transaction.

(d) <u>Violations of the Conflicts-of-Interest Policy</u>.

    (1) If the board or committee has reasonable cause to believe that a member has failed to disclose actual or possible conflicts of interest, it shall inform the member of the basis for such belief and afford the member an opportunity to explain the alleged failure to disclose.

    (2) If, after hearing the response of the member and making such further investigation as may be warranted in the circumstances, the board or committee determines that the member has in fact failed to disclose an actual or possible conflict of interest, it shall take appropriate disciplinary and corrective action.

4. <u>Records of Proceedings</u>. The minutes of the board and all committees with board authority shall contain-

    (a) the names of the persons who disclosed or otherwise were found to have a financial interest in connection with a transaction or arrangement, and the nature of the financial interest; and

    (b) the names of the persons who were present for discussions and votes relating to the transaction or arrangement, the content of the discussion, including any alternatives to the proposed transaction or arrangement, and a record of any votes taken in connection therewith.

5. <u>Compensation Committees</u>. A voting member of the board of directors, or of any committee whose jurisdiction includes compensation matters, and who receives compensation, directly or indirectly, from the Corporation for services is precluded from discussing and voting on matters pertaining to that member's compensation. However, such a person is not prohibited from providing information to the board of directors or any committee regarding compensation of similarly situated persons.

6. <u>Annual Statements</u>. Each director, principal officer and member of a committee with board delegated powers shall annually sign a statement which affirms that such person-

    (a) has received a copy of this conflicts of interest policy;

(b) has read and understands the policy;

(c) has agreed to comply with the policy; and

(d) understands that the Corporation is a charitable organization and that in order to maintain its federal tax exemption it must engage primarily in activities which accomplish one or more of its tax-exempt purposes.

7. <u>Periodic Reviews</u>. To ensure that the Corporation operates in a manner consistent with its charitable purposes and that it does not engage in activities that could jeopardize its status as an organization exempt from federal income tax, periodic reviews shall be conducted. The periodic reviews shall, at a minimum, include the following subjects:

(a) whether compensation arrangements and benefits are reasonable and are consistent with the results of arm's-length bargaining;

(b) whether acquisitions of goods or services result in inurement or impermissible private benefit;

(c) whether partnership and joint venture arrangements conform to written policies, are properly recorded, reflect reasonable payments for goods and services, further the Corporation's charitable purposes and do not result in inurement or impermissible private benefit; and

(d) whether agreements to provide goods or services further the Corporation's charitable purposes and do not result in inurement or impermissible private benefit.

8. <u>Use of Outside Experts</u>. In conducting the periodic reviews provided for in Section 7, the Corporation may, but need not, use outside advisors. If outside experts are used, their use shall not relieve the board of its responsibility for ensuring that periodic reviews are conducted.

Appendix C

--- - - ---

SAMPLE EXECUTIVE
COMPENSATION-SETTING POLICY

As with any significant policy, an organization should consult with legal counsel in adopting a policy covering the topics addressed herein.

Section 1.01. <u>Setting and approval of key executive employee compensation arrangements</u>. Compensation arrangements of key executive employees of the Corporation shall be approved in advance by an authorized body (as defined in Section 1.03) of the Corporation who shall have obtained and relied upon appropriate data as to comparability (as defined in Section 1.04) prior to making its determination. The authorized body shall adequately document (as defined in Section 1.05) the basis for its determination concurrently with making that determination.

Section 1.02 <u>Key executive employee</u>. For purposes of this policy, the term "key executive employee" includes the officers and directors of the Corporation and any individual who has powers and responsibilities similar to officers and directors of the Corporation. The term includes any person who, regardless of title, has ultimate responsibility for implementing the decisions of the Board, for supervising the management, administration, or operation of the Corporation as a whole, or for managing the finances of the Corporation as a whole. The term does not include the heads of separate departments or smaller units of the Corporation, as these individuals do not have management responsibilities for the Corporation as a whole.

Section 1.03 <u>Authorized body</u>. The term "authorized body" shall, with respect to the CEO or top management official of the Corporation, include the Board of Directors of the Corporation or a committee of the Board of Directors, which may be composed of any individuals permitted under state law or the Corporation's By-laws to serve on such a committee, to the extent that the committee is permitted by State law to act on behalf of the Board of Directors. However, such authorized body shall be composed solely of individuals who do not have a conflict of interest (as defined in Section 1.04) with respect to such compensation arrangement.

With respect to key executive employees other than the CEO or top management official, the authorized body consists solely of the CEO, who is authorized by the Board of Directors to establish such compensation, provided that the CEO does not have a conflict of interest (as defined in Section 1.04) with respect to such compensation arrangement. In the event that the CEO has a conflict of interest with respect to any key executive employee, the authorized body with respect to that employee shall be the authorized body described in the preceding paragraph.

Section 1.04   Absence of conflict of interest.   A member of the governing body authorized to approve key executive employee compensation arrangements does not have a conflict of interest with respect to a compensation arrangement only if the member:

(a) Is not a disqualified person (within the meaning of Treas. Reg. §53.4958-3) participating in or economically benefiting from the compensation arrangement, and is not a member of the family (as defined in Treas. Reg. §53.4958-3(b)(1)) of any such disqualified person;

(b) Is not in an employment relationship subject to the direction or control of any disqualified person participating in or economically benefiting from the compensation arrangement;

(c) Does not receive compensation or other payments subject to approval by any disqualified person participating in or economically benefiting from the compensation arrangement;

(d) Has no material financial interest affected by the compensation arrangement; and

(e) Does not approve a transaction providing economic benefits to any disqualified person participating in the compensation arrangement, who in turn has approved or will approve a transaction providing economic benefits to the member.

Section 1.05 – Appropriate data as to comparability. The authorized body has appropriate data as to comparability if, given the knowledge and expertise of its members, it has information sufficient to determine whether the compensation arrangement in its entirety is reasonable.   Relevant information shall include, but is not limited to, compensation levels paid by similarly situated organizations, both taxable and tax-exempt, for functionally comparable positions; the availability of similar services in the geographic area of the Corporation; current compensation surveys compiled by independent firms; and actual written offers from similar institutions competing for the services of the individual for whom the compensation arrangement is being set. Updated comparability data should be obtained by the authorized body on a periodic basis, generally at least every three years. However, more frequent updates of comparability data should be obtained if annual compensation increases exceed a modest percentage in keeping with increases generally applicable to all employees.

Section 1.06 <u>Adequate documentation</u>. The written or electronic records of the authorized body shall note:

(a) The terms of the compensation arrangement that was approved and the date it was approved;

(b) The members of the authorized body who were present during debate on the compensation arrangement that was approved and those who voted on it;

(c) The comparability data obtained and relied upon by the authorized body and how the data was obtained; and

(d) Any actions taken with respect to consideration of the compensation arrangement by anyone who is otherwise a member of the authorized body but who had a conflict of interest with respect to the compensation arrangement.

If the authorized body determines that reasonable compensation for a specific arrangement is higher than the range of comparability data obtained, the authorized body must record the basis for its determination.

The documentation outlined in the section shall be duly recorded in the minutes of the authorized body before the later of the next meeting of the authorized body or 60 days after the final action or actions of the authorized body are taken. Such records shall be reviewed and approved by the authorized body as reasonable, accurate and complete within a reasonable time period thereafter.

Appendix D

—————————— - - ——————————

Sample Policy on Dishonesty, Fraud, and Whistleblower Protection

As with any significant policy, an organization should consult with legal counsel in adopting a policy covering the topics addressed herein.

[Name of Organization Here]

(In the sample document, the word "Organization" should be replaced as appropriate with the name of the Organization.)

Standards of Conduct

Organization requires that all persons covered by this policy adhere to and follow standards of conduct that are ethical, honest, and above reproach. The reputation of Organization is of paramount importance, and Organization expects all persons covered by this policy to govern themselves accordingly. To be clear, Organization prohibits persons covered by this policy from engaging in any conduct that is dishonest, fraudulent, or illegal.

Important Note for Certain Religious, Charitable, and Humanitarian Relief Organizations

In some cases, nonprofit organizations take calculated risks and engage in activities in certain countries or jurisdictions where such activities are illegal or otherwise prohibited. For example, some oppressive government regimes prohibit certain exercise of religious activity, certain educational activity, or even providing humanitarian relief to certain persons. Organizations engaging in religious, educational, or charitable activities that may violate the laws of such oppressive regimes may wish to consider, under the advice of their legal counsel, tempering the language in this policy that prohibits "illegal" activity. For example, an organization may wish to consider language such as the following: Notwithstanding Organization's policy generally prohibiting illegal activity, Organization takes into consideration its mandate to carry out its mission when conducting activities in locations governed by oppressive regimes with laws that prohibit the free exercise of religion, education, or humanitarian relief.

COVERED PERSONS

This policy covers directors, officers, and employees of Organization. When Organization contracts with parties other than Covered Persons to perform services for Organization, Organization officials responsible for establishing and overseeing the contractual relationship shall determine, using reasonable and prudent judgment, the extent to which the principles of this policy should be incorporated into the contractual relationship.

ETHICS AND COMPLIANCE OFFICER

The board of directors of Organization has established that the _____ *[title of person designated – e.g., CEO]* of Organization serves at the Ethics and Compliance Officer for purposes of this policy.

REPORTING

If you are a Covered Person under this policy, you may report violations or suspected violations directly to the Ethics and Compliance Officer, who may be contacted by _____ *[describe method of contact]*. In the event that your concerns relate to the Ethics and Compliance Officer or you have a good faith reason to believe that your concerns will not be appropriately considered by the Ethics and Compliance Officer, you may report your concerns to the _____, *[provide alternate reporting option – e.g., chair of the board of directors]*, who may be contacted by _____ *[describe method of contact]*. Organization encourages any person covered by this policy who observes a violation or suspected violation of this policy to report the matter as promptly as possible for the benefit and protection of Organization.

GOOD FAITH

Any person reporting a violation or suspected violation of this policy must do so having a good faith belief that a violation has occurred or may have occurred. Reporting a matter as a violation or suspected violation that is known by the reporting person to be false is, itself, a violation of this policy, and shall subject the falsely reporting party to appropriate disciplinary action.

CONFIDENTIALITY

[Address with legal counsel the extent to which confidentiality should be addressed in your organization's policy. There are competing forces to consider. For example, should the policy permit reporting of a matter anonymously? To what extent should the policy state that the organization will take precautions to

protect the identity of the reporting party? (Keep in mind that the organization may not be able to protect the person's identity in some circumstances.) Due to such very important legal considerations, the author has not included proposed language in the sample policy for confidentiality. In fact, an organization may decide, under the advice of legal counsel, not to include any provision in the policy related to expectations of confidentiality.]

INVESTIGATION

The Ethics and Compliance Officer shall, under the advice of legal counsel, perform an appropriate investigation of all matters reported under this policy and respond appropriately. The Ethics and Compliance Officer shall timely inform the board of directors of each complaint or report of a violation or suspected violation, together with its status until resolved. For matters reported to _____ *[the alternate reporting option in the preceding paragraph]*, the _____ *[the alternate reporting option in the preceding paragraph]* shall, under the advice of legal counsel, perform the investigation, respond appropriately, and inform the board of directors accordingly.

NO RETALIATION

Organization expressly prohibits retaliation of any type against persons covered by this policy for reporting a violation or suspected violation in good faith or for cooperating in any investigation of a reported matter. Any employee, officer, or director engaging in prohibited retaliation shall be subject to appropriate disciplinary action up to and including termination of employment or office. Any person covered by this policy who believes he or she has been subjected to prohibited retaliation should immediately report the incident to the Ethics and Compliance Officer as described above.

CONFLICTS OF INTEREST PROHIBITED

No party who is implicated in a reported violation or suspected violation shall serve in any role related to directing the investigation of such matter or determining the appropriate response of Organization with respect to such matter.

Appendix E

————————— - - —————————

SAMPLE DONOR PRIVACY POLICY

As with any significant policy, an organization should consult with legal counsel in adopting a policy covering the topics addressed herein.

XYZ Organization is committed to respecting the privacy of our donors. We have developed this privacy policy to ensure our donors that donor information will not be shared with any third party.

AWARENESS

XYZ Organization provides this Donor Privacy Policy to make you aware of our privacy policy, and to inform you of the way your information is used. We also provide you with the opportunity to remove your name from our distribution or mailing list, if you desire to do so.

INFORMATION COLLECTED

Here are the types of donor information that we collect and maintain:

- Contact information: name, organization, complete address, phone number, email address;

- Payment information: credit card number, expiration date, and billing information;

- Shipping information: name, organization, complete address;

- Information concerning how you heard about XYZ Organization;

- Information you wish to share: questions, comments, suggestions; and

- Your request to receive periodic communications (for example, periodic fund-raising appeals, newsletters, or other communications)

153

HOW INFORMATION IS USED

XYZ Organization uses your information to serve you and to provide you with information about XYZ Organization. Credit card numbers are used only for donation or payment processing. We use the comments you offer to provide you with information requested, and we take seriously each recommendation as to how we might improve communication.

NO SHARING OF PERSONAL INFORMATION

XYZ Organization does not sell, rent, or lease your personal information to other organizations. Donor information is used solely to carrying out the activities and purposes of XYZ Organization.

REMOVING YOUR NAME FROM OUR DISTRIBUTION LIST

It is our desire to not send unwanted communications to our donors. Please contact us if you wish to be removed from our distribution list.

CONTACTING US

If you have comments or questions about our donor privacy policy, please send us an email at info@XYZOrganization.org or call us at (XXX) XXX-XXXX.

———————— - - ————————

This sample policy was derived from a model document created by ECFA, a national organization providing independent accreditation for certain religious nonprofit organizations in the areas of governance and financial integrity. The model document was used by the author to create this sample policy with ECFA's permission. Information about ECFA may be obtained at www.ecfa.org.

Appendix F

SAMPLE GIFT ACCEPTANCE POLICY

As with any significant policy, an organization should consult with legal counsel in adopting a policy covering the topics addressed herein.

DONOR-RESTRICTED CASH GIFTS

Cash gifts over $10,000 that are given with a donor restriction (other than gifts to a special fund already approved by the Board of Directors) must be brought before the Board of Directors for approval prior to acceptance. Recommendations for special recognition of donors (such as publicizing names, naming buildings, rooms, etc.) will be referred to the Board for approval. For donor-restricted cash gifts approved by the Board of Directors and exceeding $100,000, the President shall ensure that the Organization's legal counsel assists in the drafting or review of the documents constituting the gift transfer.

The President or his/her designee is responsible for addressing proposed donor-restricted cash gifts of $10,000 or less where the proposed restriction is not to a fund already approved by the Board of Directors. Such gifts, if accepted, must be for purposes consistent with the Organization's mission and must involve complete expenditure of the gifts within one year of receipt.

GIFTS OF NONCASH PROPERTY

Receiving gifts of noncash property can result in additional expenses for the Organization. This policy establishes a minimum standard for matters to be reviewed in making the determination of whether to accept or reject a gift of noncash property. Once a gift of property is accepted, a proper acknowledgment that conforms to current federal tax law shall be provided to the donor.

REAL PROPERTY

Prior to accepting a gift of real property, the President or his/her designee shall perform an initial evaluation of the practicality of accepting the offered donation. If the initial evaluation is positive, the President or his/her designee shall oversee the performance of reasonable due diligence, including assessment of environmental matters, title, and other such matters deemed appropriate by the President or his/her designee under the advice of legal counsel. The President or his/her designee will make a recommendation to the Board of Directors regarding acceptance of the donation. The Board must approve, in advance, acceptance of real property. The President or his/her designee shall ensure that the Organization's legal counsel assists in the drafting or review of the documents constituting the gift transfer.

INTANGIBLE PERSONAL PROPERTY

The President or his/her designee shall address proposed gifts of intangible personal property as follows, provided, however, that contributions with donor restrictions are subject to the policy on donor-restricted cash gifts as set forth above. Contributions of publicly traded securities with a ready market may be accepted and should be sold as soon as possible after receipt. Contributions of other types of intangible personal property including, but not limited to, stock in privately-held entities, limited liability company membership interests, partnership interests, or private debt instruments, must first be evaluated for potential value and marketability. If the President or his/her designee believes the potential value and marketability of a proposed gift warrants further consideration, he/she shall consult with legal counsel and tax counsel as necessary to evaluate the implications of accepting the gift. If the President or his/her designee, after such consultations, considers it desirable to pursue acceptance of the proposed gift, he/she shall present his/her findings and recommendations to the Board of Directors for final approval prior to acceptance of the proposed gift. Except in the case of a transfer of publicly traded securities with a ready market, the President or his/her designee shall ensure that the Organization's legal counsel assists in the drafting or review of the documents constituting the gift transfer.

TANGIBLE PERSONAL PROPERTY

Prior to accepting a gift of tangible personal property, the President or his/her designee shall perform an initial evaluation of the practicality of accepting the offered donation. If the initial evaluation is positive, the President or his/her designee shall oversee the performance of reasonable due diligence.

(a) Tangible personal property will be accepted only if:

    (i) The property is in good condition and can be used by the Organization in its mission; or

    (ii) The property can be sold for an amount adequate to exceed costs associated with accepting, holding and disposing of the gift.

(b) Tangible personal property having a value of $5,000 or more shall be accepted only after the President or his/her designee has consulted with legal counsel to address risks of unpaid liens or other liabilities taking into consideration possible UCC-1 lien searches or similar lien searches.

(c) All gifts of tangible personal property valued at more than $1,000 must be approved by the President or his/her designee before they can be accepted. Any tangible personal property gifts valued over $10,000 also require approval of the Board of Directors prior to acceptance. For gifts of tangible personal property valued at more than $100,000, the President or his/her designee shall ensure that the Organization's legal counsel assists in the drafting or review of the documents constituting the gift transfer.

Appendix G

————— - - —————

SAMPLE EXPENSE REIMBURSEMENT POLICY

As with any significant policy, an organization should consult with legal counsel in adopting a policy covering the topics addressed herein.

PURPOSE

The Board of Directors of [name of organization] recognizes that board members, officers, and employees of [name of organization] may be required to travel or incur other expenses from time to time to conduct organization business and to further the mission of this nonprofit organization. The purpose of this Policy is (a) to ensure that appropriate cost considerations apply, (b) to ensure that expenditures are appropriate, and (c) to provide a uniform and consistent approach for the timely reimbursement of authorized expenses incurred by Employees. It is the policy of [name of organization] to reimburse only reasonable and necessary expenses actually incurred by employees.

When incurring business expenses, [name of organization] expects employees to:

- Exercise discretion and good business judgment with respect to expenses incurred;

- Be cost-conscious and spend organization money as carefully and judiciously as the individual would spend his or her own funds; and

- Report expenses, supported by required documentation, as they were actually spent.

EXPENSE REPORTS

Expenses will not be reimbursed unless the individual requesting reimbursement submits a written Expense Report following current guidelines. The Expense Report, which shall be submitted at least monthly or within two weeks of the completion of travel if travel expense reimbursement is requested, must include:

- The individual's name;

- For travel, the date, origin, destination and purpose of the trip, including a description of each organization-related activity during the trip;

- The name and affiliation of all people for whom expenses are claimed (i.e., people on whom money is spent in order to conduct [name of organization]'s business); and

- An itemized list of all expenses for which reimbursement is requested.

RECEIPTS

No expense in excess of $___ will be reimbursed unless the employee requesting reimbursement submits with the Expense Report written receipts from each vendor (not a credit card receipt or statement) showing the vendor's name, a description of the services provided (if not otherwise obvious), the date, and the total expenses. Modest and reasonable cash expenditures for which obtaining a receipt is impracticable (e.g., cash tips, mass transit fare, etc.) may be documented by providing written itemization of such expenditures.

ORGANIZATION CREDIT CARDS

If a corporate credit card is issued to an employee for organization-related expenses, the requirements for regular expense reports, with required documentation for all charges, as described above under "Expense Reports" must still be met, and charges may not be made for "Non-reimbursable Expenditures" as described below.

GENERAL TRAVEL REQUIREMENTS

Necessity of Travel. In determining the whether travel is necessary and appropriate, those involved in the decision-making process shall consider the ways in which [name of organization] will benefit from the travel and weigh those benefits against the anticipated costs of the travel. Decision-makers should also consider whether the intended objectives may be accomplished without travel (e.g., by handling matters by phone or video meeting.)

Personal and Spousal Travel Expenses. Individuals traveling on behalf of [name of organization] may incorporate personal travel or business with their organization-related trips; however, employees shall not arrange organization travel at a time that is less advantageous to [name of organization] or that involves greater expenses to [name of organization] in order to accommodate personal travel plans. Any additional expenses incurred as a result of personal travel, including but not limited to extra hotel nights, additional stopovers, meals or transportation, are the responsibility of the individual and will not be reimbursed by [name of organization]. Expenses associated with travel of an individual's spouse, family member, or other companion will not be reimbursed by [name of organization] unless there is a "bona fide business purpose" for the companion's travel (as that term is defined under federal tax law) and reimbursement for the companion's travel costs are approved in writing in advance by an appropriate organization official.

AIR TRAVEL

General. Air travel reservations should be made as far in advance as possible in order to take advantage of reduced fares. Care should be taken to reasonably minimize additional fees such as baggage fees, change fees, etc.

Frequent Flyer Miles and Compensation for Denied Boarding. Employees traveling on behalf of [name of organization] may accept and retain frequent flyer miles and compensation for denied boarding for their personal use. Individuals may not deliberately patronize a single airline to accumulate frequent flyer miles if less expensive comparable tickets are available on another airline.

LODGING

Employees traveling on behalf of [name of organization] may be reimbursed at the single room rate for the reasonable cost of hotel accommodations. Convenience, the cost of staying in the city in which the hotel is located, and proximity to other venues on the individual's itinerary shall be considered in determining reasonableness. Employees shall make use of available corporate and discount rates for hotels.

OUT-OF-TOWN MEALS

Employees traveling on behalf of [name of organization] are reimbursed for the reasonable and actual costs of meals (including tips) subject to a maximum per diem meal allowance of $___ per day and the terms and conditions established by [name of organization] relating to the per diem meal allowance.

GROUND TRANSPORTATION

Employees are expected to use the most economical ground transportation that is reasonable and appropriate under the circumstances.

Courtesy Cars and Shuttles. Many hotels have courtesy cars and shuttles, which will take you to and from the airport at no charge. Employees should take advantage of this free service whenever feasible.

Rental Cars. Car rentals are expensive, so other forms of transportation should be considered when practical. Employees will be allowed to rent a car while out of town provided that the cost is reasonable under the circumstances. The organization does not reimburse for loss damage waivers or other additional insurance coverages. Each employee who travels and utilizes rental cars is expected to maintain automobile insurance coverage that covers their rental car usage.

PERSONAL CARS

Employees are compensated for use of their personal cars when used for organization business. When an employee uses a personal car for travel, including travel to and from the airport, mileage will be allowed at the currently approved IRS rate per mile.

In the case of individuals using their personal cars to take a trip that would normally be made by air, mileage will be allowed at the currently approved rate; however, the total mileage reimbursement will not exceed the sum of the lowest available round trip coach airfare.

PARKING/TOLLS

Parking and toll expenses, including charges for hotel parking, incurred by employees traveling on organization business will be reimbursed. The costs of parking tickets, fines, car washes, valet service, etc., are the responsibility of the employee and will not be reimbursed.

On-airport parking is permitted for short business trips. For extended trips, employees should use lower cost off-airport facilities.

ENTERTAINMENT AND BUSINESS MEETINGS

Reasonable expenses incurred for business meetings or other types of business-related entertainment will be reimbursed only if the expenditures are approved by an appropriate member of management. Detailed documentation for any such expense must be provided, including:

- Date and place of entertainment;

- Nature of expense;

- Name, titles, and corporate affiliation of those entertained;

- A complete description of the business purpose for the activity including the specific business matters discussed; and

- Vendor receipts (not credit card receipts or statements) showing the vendor's name, a description of the services provided, the date, and the total expenses, including tips (if applicable).

NON-REIMBURSABLE EXPENDITURES

Expenses deemed lavish or excessive will not be reimbursed, as such expenses are inappropriate. Expenses that are not reimbursable include:

[Organization should customize this list as appropriate]

- Travel insurance

- First class tickets or upgrades

- Limousine travel

- Alcohol

- Movies

- Recreation or golf fees

- Room service

- Club dues

- Rental or purchase of golf clubs or other sporting equipment

- Spa charges

- Clothing purchases

- Valet service

- Other activities or charges deemed lavish or extravagant by the organization's leadership

This sample policy was derived from a model document created by ECFA, a national organization providing independent accreditation for certain religious nonprofit organizations in the areas of governance and financial integrity. The model document was used by the author to create this sample policy with ECFA's permission. Information about ECFA may be obtained at www.ecfa.org.

ABOUT THE AUTHOR

Michael E. (Mike) Batts has more than 30 years of experience serving hundreds of nonprofit organizations in a variety of ways. He has served on and chaired the boards of nonprofit organizations, both nationally and locally. At the time of the book's writing, Mike serves as chairman of the board of ECFA, a national organization that accredits religious nonprofit organizations in the areas of board governance and financial integrity. He advises nonprofit organizations on matters related to board governance, financial reporting, tax compliance and strategy, risk management, corporate structure, international activities, and related topics. Mike has actively engaged in nonprofit legislative matters at the federal and state levels. He served as chairman of the Commission on Accountability and Policy for Religious Organizations, a national commission convened by ECFA upon the request of U.S. Senator Charles Grassley, to provide policy advice to Congress, the Treasury Department, the Internal Revenue Service, and the nonprofit sector related to federal tax policy affecting religious and other nonprofit organizations.

Mike recently co-authored, together with attorney and CPA Richard Hammar, the book *Church Finance* – a "go-to" reference that provides practical guidance for church financial administration. Mike has also authored three additional books, entitled *Board Member Orientation*, *Unrelated Business Income and the Church*, and *Unrelated Business Income and the 501(c)(3) Public Charity.* He is also an advisory board member of The Exempt Organization Tax Review, a leading national publication addressing tax issues in the nonprofit sector.

Mike is a CPA and the managing partner of Batts Morrison Wales & Lee, P.A., a national CPA firm headquartered in Orlando, Florida, dedicated exclusively to serving nonprofit organizations and their affiliates across the United States.

Mike speaks throughout the country and writes frequently on topics related to the nonprofit sector. He is also active legislatively, having drafted and lobbied successfully for a number of changes to laws affecting nonprofit organizations.

Made in the USA
Coppell, TX
09 February 2021

49954132R00098